IN SEARCH OF A BEGINNING

IN SEARCH OF
A BEGINNING

My Life with Graham Greene

YVONNE CLOETTA

As told to Marie-Françoise Allain

*Translated from the French
by Euan Cameron*

BLOOMSBURY

First published in Great Britain 2004

Copyright © 2004 The Estate of Yvonne Cloetta and Marie-Françoise Allain
Translation copyright © 2004 Euan Cameron
Front and back photographs of Graham Greene © J. B. Diederich

The moral right of the authors and translator has been asserted

Bloomsbury Publishing Plc, 38 Soho Square, London W1D 3HB

A CIP catalogue record for this book
is available from the British Library

ISBN 0 7475 7108 2

10 9 8 7 6 5 4 3 2 1

All papers used by Bloomsbury Publishing are natural, recyclable
products made from wood grown in well-managed forests.
The manufacturing processes conform to the
environmental regulations of the country of origin.

Typeset by Hewer Text Ltd, Edinburgh
Printed by Clays Ltd, St Ives plc

CONTENTS

Foreword

On 17 May 1989, as he handed me a copy of the first volume of Norman Sherry's biography, Graham said with a sad and gloomy expression, 'Poor you, I am afraid the day will come when you have to face some biographers. If I may give you any advice, this is what I would suggest: either you refuse to speak to them altogether – it's your right – or you agree to talk to them. If so, do tell the truth, but don't take a middle course.' (By this he meant to put me on my guard against any temptation to give a false or bowdlerised version of our relationship.)

The years have passed; I have reflected long and hard on these words.

After his death, on 3 April 1991, my initial reaction – I would almost say it was a reflex – was, of course, to say nothing and, selfishly, to keep all the many memories that had accumulated over the course of our thirty-two years together to myself. But the storm of hostility unleashed against him during the summer of 1994, a veritable smear campaign generated even by some of his 'friends', triggered such feelings of revulsion in me that I could no longer bear to maintain my silence, and so I have departed from what had always been our watchword in common: absolute discretion.

My purpose is not to respond to the accusations of his detractors – what would be the point? – but to present, with the support of precise facts, without bias or complacency, a portrait of the man I knew.

In order to compensate for any possible lapses of memory, and for the sake of truth and authenticity, I shall refer as frequently as possible to a private notebook (my *Carnet rouge*) which I kept throughout those years. Graham read this note-book on a number of occasions and annotated it in his own hand. Of course, it is merely a pale reflection of our casual conversations, without any explanations or embellishments; it is a snapshot of Graham Greene as he really was. My own title for it was 'A little of what he told me'.

Once my mind was made up, I called upon Marie-Françoise Allain to help me realise my project. Soizic, as she is known (diminutive for Françoise in Breton), is the daughter of Gra-ham's old friend the Resistance hero Yves Allain, as well as the author of *The Other Man: Conversations with Graham Greene* (London: Bodley Head, 1983), and she immediately struck me as the ideal person to accompany me along a path which is arduous and scattered with pitfalls. I am deeply grateful to her for agreeing to do so.

Yvonne Cloetta
Vevey, November 1999

Introduction

One day in April 1991, just after Graham Greene's death, Yvonne discovered, hidden away in a drawer, a short note written in shaky handwriting which simply said, 'In Search of a Beginning'.

Needless to say, she pondered on this enigmatic phrase a great deal. Was it, she asked herself, the title of a book Graham intended to write? Yet he must have known very well that he would never be able to write it. Was it not, instead, the expression of a metaphysical attempt to guess at what happens when a man, in the solitude of his final moments, knows that he will have to confront death and – if he is a believer – eternity?

Whatever the answer may be, there was the material for a search. Graham bequeathed it to his companion of some thirty-two years: material weighed down with questions, with uncertainties and effort, but also with certainties and even moments of joy. This became Yvonne's search, a quest at once modest yet ambitious: to go and join Graham, 'who looks down on us', in the beyond, from the top of that star (she says it is Jupiter) which she points to in the sky above Vevey. To rediscover Graham in practical terms, here on earth, or rather, as she came to admit after two years of our working together, to compensate for his unbearable absence; the best means of doing this was to talk freely at last, to write down and reconstruct, if only in part, all that she had had the good fortune to know and share with him. To try in some way to bring him back to life again. That life of a writer which is always so mysterious and so complicated, as well as the apparently much simpler day-to-day life of the man she knew.

At the point where these two separate elements meet, we encounter, in flesh and blood, Yvonne, the tiny Breton woman whom Graham Greene had met in Africa. Her life, too, is important. For she was utterly transformed by Graham, during his own lifetime, and the effects live on, beyond the grave. After so many years of exceptional mutual understanding, he said to her in April 1990, a year before his death, 'I now realise that love – real, true love – between two human beings only reveals itself once it's no longer a question of sex.'

A curious remark . . . In fact, it was one of the last and most touching declarations of his love for Yvonne ('He was not speaking directly about us,' Yvonne added, 'but it was a declaration of love'). Graham seemed to be attributing a sort of purity to this 'human love, ordinary and corrupted',* a nostalgia for which he, in the 1940s, had conferred on one of his characters, linking it, as is often the case in fiction, to his private life. But in 1990 Graham Greene was not returning to his former fantasies or to the romantic love affairs he had as a young man. He was expressing a feeling of achievement. He was supplying the proof of a serenity that could derive only, in fact, from long years of shared physical love. Implicit in what Yvonne had to say is the proposition 'Can true love exist without there being, or having once been, sexual involvement?' It is this, among other things, that we should understand in the course of her otherwise very discreet account.

Graham Greene was a man of passionate extremes which, miraculously, he learnt to channel through his writing. What is so striking in the portrait presented by Yvonne is the stubborn strength of his feelings – and his desire – for Yvonne. What is

* *The End of the Affair.*

Introduction

also remarkable is the echo they found in her; for without the deeply felt, sincere and totally disinterested response which Yvonne's still painful memories lay bare over the years, through the moments of separation and disappearance – without this love of Yvonne's, now finally disclosed – an entire facet of the man, and therefore the writer, would be concealed from us.

Of course, our understanding of Graham Greene is filtered – and perhaps necessarily so – through the understanding that Yvonne (who was not his alter ego, but his companion) also has of Graham Greene the writer. Without her 'fairness' and her delicate, intuitive ability to understand him, we might venture to conclude that the complicity that endured between them throughout thirty-two years could not have developed.

Yvonne Cloetta has never been the 'warrior's rest'. She has never been a 'muse' in any sense. She has been a loving woman and a beloved one. A woman.

This portrait of Graham Greene is an expression of ultimate love. It is unadorned and authentic. If credibility is to be expected, it is very much from an account of this kind that it will come, one which is neither biography nor autobiography but a straightforward narrative of a life. Meanwhile, his work lives on.

Marie-Françoise Allain

I

The Encounter

Soizic: There is a recurrent note in Graham's letters to you over the long years you spent together. He wrote, 'I love you for ever', which later became, 'I love you for ever – and a day', and then: 'I love you for ever – and the longest day', meaning eternity. In his mind, there was no end. But what about the beginning, Yvonne? Tell me about the beginning.

Yvonne: It was totally unexpected. It happened in Douala, in Cameroon. A Saturday in early March 1959, when I suddenly received a telephone call from a friend of mine, Hô Bouccarut, who said, 'Our friend Graham Greene is *de passage* in Douala. Would you care to join us for dinner tonight?' Unfortunately, I was unavailable, and so I expressed my regrets to her, but added, 'If there's one man I should like to meet, it is him.' I had seen the film *The Third Man* and read some of his books, among which *The Power and the Glory* impressed me so deeply that it had occurred to me to wonder about the sort of man who could have written such a mighty novel. Hô sounded very disappointed, but there was nothing I could do.

No rumours about Graham Greene's visit to Douala had filtered through to me, and at first I thought it might have been a joke. But on Monday morning, Hô rang up again and asked whether she could bring him over to my house for a drink. I agreed, of course, and that is how I came to find myself sitting opposite a man who was at that time nothing more to me than the author of a few books I had read and admired.

On this first encounter we were both stiff and shy. Fortunately, Hô was there to help the conversation flow. I remember that she talked about an extraordinary helicopter trip she and Graham had made the previous night, flying over Mount Cameroon. The volcano, which had been dormant for ages, had suddenly erupted. It had been a spectacular and awe-inspiring experience, and it left a deep impression on Graham.

Soizic: What brought Graham to Douala in March 1959?

Yvonne: As I discovered later on, he had just spent six weeks in a leper colony near Coquilhatville in the former Belgian Congo. It so happened that in Douala there was a man by the name of Moret whom Graham had known well during the early 1950s in Saigon, where Moret had been head of security during the French war in Indochina. The two friends had corresponded, and Moret had invited Graham to stop in Douala on his way back to England. Unfortunately, on the eve of Graham's arrival in Douala, Moret had a serious car accident on a track in the bush, and he had had to be flown back to France.

Before Moret boarded the plane on a stretcher, he had left the Bouccaruts with instructions about Graham's visit to Douala. Hô and Paul had also worked in Indochina during the French war. Hô was born in Tonkin. Paul was a French government official who worked with Moret in Saigon. The war had ended in 1955, and a number of French civil servants had been transferred from Indochina to Cameroon.

Douala was then a quiet, peaceful place, where my husband, Jacques, and I had spent happy and carefree days. In that same year of 1959, the Cameroon's imminent move towards independence was about to alter life in the country considerably – to say nothing of our own lives, of course.

But to return to Graham's short visit to Douala. In spite of the chilling information that was reaching us over the radio about the fate of the colonial population – there were incidents in which people were found dead in ditches, for example – and in spite of the mood of instability in town, the Bouccaruts were determined to celebrate Graham's presence in Douala. The best way they could think of doing so was to ask their friends to join them for an evening's dancing at the only nightclub for Europeans in Douala. This was how we came to find ourselves, that Monday night, dancing at the Chantaco until four in the morning. It obviously wasn't Graham's cup of tea: he never liked dancing anyway and, moreover, after all those weeks in a leper colony, he seemed completely lost.

Early in the morning, before our little group dispersed, Paul said to me, 'Graham is leaving tonight, and he would like the two of us to come and have a farewell drink with him at the bar of his hotel, Les Cocotiers. I'll come and fetch you at about four o'clock this afternoon, OK?' Before I could answer, he had left.

Some hours later, in the afternoon, I was woken from my siesta by Paul Bouccarut's voice saying, 'Get up quickly. Graham is with me. He wants us to go back to his hotel to say goodbye.' I replied, 'But I've already said goodbye to him at the Chantaco.' Paul put his finger to his lips, for Graham was waiting in the sitting-room. Knowing what a devious go-between Paul could be, I said, 'You're a friend, aren't you? Swear that you won't leave me alone with him at the hotel.' He promised. So off we went to Les Cocotiers. Not to the bar, in fact, but up to Graham's bedroom. Graham continued with his packing, but at the same time we got involved, much to Paul's disappointment, in a serious conversation about life, death and love in general.

Graham's brief stay in Douala was coming to an end. As far as I was concerned, it was nothing more than a slightly unusual interlude which would soon be forgotten. His view of matters was different, however. Before he left, he said, 'Hô told me she'll be in Nice next August, and I gather that you'll also be in the South of France at that time. I'm returning now to England, and then I go to Cuba, and afterwards to Capri. Later on, in August, I'm supposed to spend a week with friends at La Voile d'Or in Saint-Jean-Cap-Ferrat. Would Hô and you care to join me there for an aperitif?' I replied, 'August is still a long way off. We'll see.'

I had not realised at that juncture how determined Graham was that we should see each other again. We did indeed meet for that famous aperitif with Hô, during which he asked me discreetly whether I would have dinner with him the next day at La Réserve in Beaulieu, not far from where he was staying. I accepted the invitation, and I've never regretted doing so.

Soizic: Was that such an important step?

Yvonne: Very much so. We were left alone for the first time, and we could speak at leisure.

Soizic: What was so unusual about that?

Yvonne: Nothing, really, but it was the determining factor in our future together. In March 1959, when Graham came to Douala, because the political situation was growing more and more dangerous, my husband, Jacques, and I had come to a decision that I would return to France and remain there with our two young daughters, in spite of all the anxieties this would entail. Jacques had decided that he had to stay in Africa for the sake of his career. For each of us, it meant beginning a new kind of life, which implied liberties on either side. However, the idea of remaining in France on my own with Martine and Brigitte, who were aged eight and four respectively, would mean heavy responsibilities for me, and I was very aware of them. On top of that, I had just endured a very painful experience in my personal life. During the three months that had passed since our meeting, a great deal had altered, so much so, in fact, that

Graham noticed the change straightaway. 'Between the cheerful woman I met in Douala and the one I find now, there is a great difference,' he remarked. 'Has anything happened in the meantime?'

I found myself telling him everything that was weighing on my mind. He listened to me with such deep interest and concern that by the end of the meal I had reached the conclusion that here, sitting in front of me, was someone whom I had not known two hours previously, but who now knew me better than I did myself. And that is how I came to realise that he was no ordinary man; not, as far as I was concerned, just because he was a great writer, but because of the human qualities I was discovering in him.

Soizic: All the same, Yvonne, he was already a very famous writer. Weren't you, at least initially, attracted or impressed by his celebrity? How could you avoid being seduced by his fame, however slightly?

Yvonne: It is true that the admiration I felt – which is a part of love – had probably affected me already. As to his fame, that is something exterior. I was certainly not aware of these aspects. What struck me most were his qualities of empathy, which helped him to find the exact words I needed to hear. That evening I had the feeling of having found a real friend. A man I could rely upon.

I drove him back to his hotel. We stayed in the car, looking out over the boats in the harbour of Saint-Jean, and talking and talking until dawn.

He was leaving for London the next day and he asked me whether I would drive him to Nice airport, which I did. We had lunch together at the Ciel d'Azur, high up at the top of the airport building. When the time came for him to board his plane, and as we were taking the lift down to the check-in desk, he took me in his arms and asked, '*Est-ce que tu m'aimes?*' I was somewhat astonished to be asked this so suddenly. I replied, 'I don't know. It's too early for me to tell. I can't answer your question.' Perhaps he was disappointed, but at any rate he didn't show it.

A week or so later, when he had flown over from London, he referred again to this occasion: 'In fact, it was at that very moment that I started loving you,' he said. 'I appreciated your honesty so much.' Yet at the same time, in order to save his pride, we agreed that there had been a misunderstanding about the verb *aimer* – to love – which to me, from what I had learnt at school, had a very specific meaning in English. He had actually meant to say, he confessed, 'Do you like me?'

Many, many years afterwards, in his last work of fiction, *The Captain and the Enemy*, one finds traces of that conversation: 'To love and to like – it must have been difficult for me as a child to learn how to distinguish between the two' (Ch. 3). He even returned to the theme, two months before his death, in the inscription he wrote on the back of a photograph of himself, 'I thank God that you didn't dislike me in Douala.'

And for over thirty years, each time we entered a lift together, he would take me in his arms.

2

A Burnt-Out Case?

Soizic: In 1961, in the copy of *A Burnt-Out Case* that he inscribed to you, Graham wrote, 'This book about a different Africa from yours.' Wasn't Africa, where you first met, a link between the two of you?

Yvonne: Not exactly. Geographically speaking, we didn't visit the same countries, and Africa is so very big. But the main difference lies in the ways in which we lived our lives there. I had spent fourteen years in various parts of Africa: in Dakar in Senegal, where I got married, Cotonou in Dahomey, Lomé in Togo, Bamako in Mali, and Douala in French Cameroon. On the whole, they were happy years. It was a fairly idle life, as we had a lot of servants, and social life occupied a large slice of it. My best memories, however, are of the journeys into the bush, which gave one a real feeling of adventure.

All the same, after a time one began to feel enclosed in a very narrow world – an artificial, hollow world in which cocktail parties, nightclubs, promiscuity and gossip invaded our daily lives and our minds.

As you can imagine, that was not the type of life Graham would have appreciated. His own experiences in Africa were much more exotic and perilous. His first trip to Africa in 1931, when he walked across Liberia with his cousin Barbara and a few native carriers, nearly killed him through nervous strain, exhaustion and malaria. In *Journey without Maps* (1935), he gave us an idea of just what a nightmare the crazy journey had been.

Several years after that book was published, in 1941, he went back to West Africa, to Lagos as well as to Freetown, Sierra Leone, where he stayed for eighteen months. He was on an MI6 mission there, which he described as 'government work of a rather ill-defined nature'.* In his spare time, he wrote *The Ministry of Fear* (1943), and five years later, in 1948, he published *The Heart of the Matter*, which was directly inspired by Africa.

At the beginning of March 1959, when we met in Douala, Graham was returning from a disturbing 'heart of darkness' trip to the leper colony at Yonda. He was all the more aware, therefore, of the very different ways of life the two of us had been leading in Africa, and this explains his inscription to me in *A Burnt-Out Case*.

But whatever our different experiences there, what we certainly had in common was our love for the continent that Graham used to call 'The Soup-Sweet Land': its tropical beauty; the nonchalance and kindness of the people; and our interest in their habits and superstitions, for which we both felt great sympathy. We also shared a very vivid memory of the smell of Africa: that typically pervasive flavour which was a combination of muggy heat, damp earth and the spicy scent of the natives' skins. It's a smell one cannot find anywhere else, one that you cannot forget, and which leaves behind a certain nostalgia.

Soizic: In Douala, did Graham mention his six weeks in the leper colony in Yonda?

Yvonne: Yes, he did, but without going into details, of course. But, as I explained, our preoccupations were so different . . . It

* Introduction to *In Search of a Character* (1961).

was only when we met again in the summer of that year that he told me his reason for going there. And that was also the moment when I discovered the state of mind he was in.

He was more or less a burnt-out case himself. I gradually found out that what drew him to that remote place was the need to attempt a real escape from a life he could not bear any more. As a writer, he believed he had come to an end, that his sources had dried up, and that the book he was planning to write, *A Burnt-Out Case*, would be his last. As a man, he no longer believed in anything, and certainly not in love. He had endured failure after failure: 'the long despair of doing nothing well, the cafard that hangs around a writer's life', as he expressed his disillusion at the time.

Soizic: Would you say that that particular moment of melancholy was worse or different from other ones?

Yvonne: It is difficult for me to make a comparison, since at the time I didn't know any of the details of his life before we met. All I can say is that nowhere in his work have I encountered a person as gloomy as Querry, the main character in *A Burnt-Out Case*.

Soizic: There is something I find hard to understand here. For two years, from 1959 until 1961, when the novel was published, Graham had been writing about a very depressive character; yet at the same time a love affair had developed between the two of you, and as far as that side of things was concerned he was a happy man, wasn't he? How could he cope with such a paradoxical situation?

Yvonne: Well, Soizic, here you put your finger on an important point: the relationship between the man, his real life and his work, that of writing fiction. What I can tell you is that he suffered terribly having to put up with that character Querry, who obsessed him, and with a woman whom he had started to love. He felt torn between the two, each of them being part of himself.

Soizic: Were you, Yvonne, 'part of himself'?

Yvonne: Perhaps I wasn't part of him. I was part of his life, I think. But Querry, who was a kind of alter ego, was certainly part of him. While he was writing the book, he literally 'lived' with Querry, and that depressed him terribly.

Soizic: Do you mean that he had become dominated by the character he had created?

Yvonne: That is still a mystery to me. As he observed in a conversation between the two of us which I noted down, 'Obviously, emotion has a great part in the creation of fictitious characters. The only way of giving them life is to imagine how they might react confronted with such and such a situation. This is where the emotional element comes in. To describe the impact of facts on such a character and, consequently, his reactions, I have to feel myself real, deep emotion facing the same facts, in the same situation' (*Carnet rouge*). That explains why, in this particular case, he was dragged down by Querry's depression.

Soizic: Wasn't Querry's depression his own in 'real' life?

Yvonne: No. There was, at least in those days, a *décalage* – a lag or an interval – between what he was experiencing in his imagination – still, probably, the effect of his recent experiences – and the life we were living together. I would say he had to create a wall between the two. And how he coped with that, I cannot say.

Soizic: You said he 'suffered' from it . . .

Yvonne: Immensely. He even suffered physically. I remember spending Christmas 1960 at my Italian friend Lella's house in San Remo. Graham was staying at a hotel nearby, and we all had a very pleasant dinner together. Next morning, when I met him at his hotel, he looked awful. I enquired after his health. He said he had been sick all night. 'Did anything in the food disagree with you?' I asked. 'No,' he said. 'When I came back here last night I felt I had to work a bit more on the book. Finding myself in the company of Querry, I felt so depressed that I had to vomit.'

In those days, it was very difficult for me to understand how there could be a link between writing a book and being sick. I was to learn a great deal more about it later on. Curiously enough, some years afterwards, V. S. Pritchett and his wife came to Antibes. We were all going to have lunch together at a restaurant in the old town. As we walked there, Victor and Graham talked about the job of writing. They agreed how painful it could be, and Victor admitted that quite often he felt sick after having done his day's work.

Having so often seen Graham's drawn expression as he emerged from his daily chore, I came to understand the agony he went through, even though I couldn't possibly share it. It was like a woman giving birth. What can one do to help her?

3

Ghosts of the Past

Soizic: What seems to have been an unusually strong bond of love between you endured until Graham Greene's death on 3 April 1991. In the last months of his life, he left you a message which read, 'I could not live without you.' And the very last time I met him myself, in Antibes in October 1990, when he was already very ill, I was moved by one particular remark he made to me – an intense, youthful, pathetic confession: 'If she didn't exist, I'd put a bullet through my head.'

We know all about Graham's previous turbulent love affairs, and also about his manic depressive moods. But did they ever interfere with your relationship with him?

Yvonne: Not really. I think he had learnt his lesson from the past. He knew from experience how destructive and disastrous such moods could be – jealousy, in particular – and he was determined not to put the burden on me.

All the same, once I had got to know him a bit better, I came to understand his state of mind and to realise the depths of his depressive moods. As I told you before, he was pretty much a 'burnt-out case' himself. By that I mean that, just like the lepers, he had lost a great deal of himself through painful experiences, and yet he was still alive – very much so, in fact – and he was ready to start again, although with very little hope, as he confided in me later. He was a fighter, though, and the odds must have been loaded on our side . . .

Soizic: On the whole, then, happiness is what seems to have prevailed. Would you say that your life together was 'one long, quiet stream'?

Yvonne: Long, yes, but quiet, I'm not so sure – and certainly not in the beginning.

Soizic: Why?

Yvonne: At the beginning, and for some fifteen years afterwards, there was real passion on both sides, with all that that entails: excitement, quarrels, misunderstandings . . .

Soizic: And maybe a few attempts at escape?

Yvonne: No, never. No ruptures, in any case. Only remnants of our pasts coming between us every now and then.
 Remember, Soizic, that when we met Graham was fifty-five and I was thirty-six. You alluded to his past. He once admitted to you that in his 'private life', his situation wasn't regular, that he had been 'cruel'.* But then, I hadn't exactly been an angel either . . .

Soizic: So, if I understand correctly, the passionate beginnings were a little difficult and tumultuous, were they not?

Yvonne: Well, I suppose that's normal, and it applies to everybody until one feels settled; one is overstrained, ready to explode at any moment.
 The first quarrel I can recall arose because of Catherine

---

* See *The Other Man: Conversations with Graham Greene* by Marie-Françoise Allain (London: Bodley Head, 1983).

Walston. Graham had already told me a lot about her and about their earlier love affair. We had been spending a few days together at La Voile d'Or at Saint-Jean-Cap-Ferrat. Our stay there was coming to an end and I resented him leaving and going back to London. I implored him to stay a few more days.

'But I have to go,' he said. 'I will be back soon, in four days' time.' And then he repeated what he had said: 'But at this moment, I have to go.'

'What do you have to do in London that's so important?' I asked.

'I promised Catherine I'd accompany her to a Picasso exhibition tomorrow.'

I felt as if I had been hit over the head. I reacted violently.

'Well, go, then,' I said. 'But before you come back, make up your mind. It will be her or me, but not both of us.'

Off he went, gazing at me in despair. While he was away, he rang me three times a day, just to find out how I was feeling. He swore that all this was simply a misunderstanding between us, saying, 'I will tell you the truth, I will tell you the truth.'

Four days later, when we were together again just as he had promised, I asked, 'How did it go? I mean the Picasso exhibition you went to with Catherine?'

'We quarrelled. We didn't go,' was his answer.

And then he told me the real reason for his trip to London. During the winter of 1961, he had had a bad bout of pneumonia in Moscow and it had lingered on for months. His London doctor had therefore wanted him to see a radiologist to have his lungs X-rayed. Because the results were not satisfactory – there was a dubious spot somewhere – the radiologist asked him to come back for further X-rays. Graham had postponed everything, however, and had come to join me in the south of France, convinced that he had lung cancer and that the doctor had not dared tell him the truth. Incidentally, he made use of this personal experience with his doctor in his short story 'Under the Garden'.

One can easily imagine the state of mind he was in and appreciate why he really did have to go back to London for the second X-rays. Yet he had decided not to tell me about the problem in order not to upset me.

Soizic: How did you feel then?

Yvonne: Relieved, because by the time he returned to be with me in France, we knew there was nothing seriously wrong with his health. I also felt ashamed of myself for having been unjust to him. I pointed out to him, however, that had he told me the true reason for his going back to London I would certainly have been anxious during his absence, but we would also have been spared a quarrel which nearly led to a rift.

Soizic: Because of Catherine Walston?

Yvonne: No. Apart from one or two painful occasions, Catherine Walston was not a source of friction between us. After all, he often used to say that the time he had spent with her was the most 'tormented' and 'chaotic' period of his life. To the extent that in 1965, after telling me frankly about his plans, Graham went to his villa in Capri with her. She was recovering from an accident in which she had broken her hip. Not only did I understand – his openness helped in this respect – but in a curious way I couldn't help feeling a kind of admiration and a touch of sympathy for his wanting to do this and for being so concerned about someone he had once loved.

Soizic: Do you mean you weren't jealous?

Yvonne: No, certainly not of his past. Only the present mattered to me. And I was proved right, for while he was in Capri he wrote to me, in a letter dated 11 July 1965, 'I'm really glad I've done this for her.' That remark speaks more of concern than of love. In the same letter, he added, 'Catherine told me I should take you to Anacapri.' It was another two years before he asked me to accompany him to Anacapri. That was in 1967.

Soizic: Why did he wait so long?

Yvonne: Because he was afraid I would find 'ghosts' there, as he put it. He was remembering a painful episode which took place in London when I visited his rooms in Albany for the first time in 1963. I certainly encountered a ghost there, when I discovered a large photograph of Catherine on his bedside table. That was a shock, and he suddenly became a stranger to me. When I left England after that visit, I really thought I had seen the last of him.

Soizic: How did it happen that the photograph was still there, four years after your first meeting?

Yvonne: The only explanation he could give me was: 'I was not aware of that photo being there . . .' It took some time, and many discussions, before he managed to convince me – and I remain convinced to this day – that Catherine Walston belonged to the past.

Soizic: Weren't you a bit naive, however, in those days?

Yvonne: It wasn't naivety. But then I knew enough about how he functioned to feel secure. What is more, I had no choice: I just cannot distrust a man I love.

Soizic: Knowing 'how he functioned'. In the case of a character like Graham Greene's, was that not virtually impossible to do?

Yvonne: It certainly was. So much so that after having been with him for thirty-two years I still couldn't claim to have known him thoroughly . . . But we were discussing Graham Greene's relationships with women . . . From what he had told me about his past, I was certain of one thing, at least: he always had great difficulty in making up his mind and bringing a love affair to an end; but once he had made a decision, it was irrevocable, and he would not turn back on it. This is what I meant when I used the words 'how he functioned', and it was certainly true as far as Catherine Walston was concerned.

I should like to add something at this point: whenever he talked about women he had loved in the past, he never spoke badly of them or told me anything that was unkind. In fact, he always remained on friendly terms with them.

Soizic: As you came to discover more about the man, were there aspects of his personality which upset you or which you disliked?

Yvonne: Yes, there were. Right at the very beginning there was one obnoxious aspect of his past that came as something of a shock.

In the late summer of 1959, we went to Paris together for the first time, to stay at the Hotel St James and Albany. One evening he invited a friend of mine, Emmy de C., for dinner at L'Auberge Sainte-Anne, overlooking Notre-Dame. The three of us were in a cheerful mood, the restaurant was very pleasant, and the food was delicious, not to mention the wines . . .

After dinner, Graham asked Emmy and me what we would like to do. We had no idea, so we left the decision to him. He ordered a taxi and asked the driver to drop us at the near end of the rue de Douai. Neither of us had ever heard about that particular Paris street. As soon as we got out of the cab, a man dressed in a bizarre sort of uniform pounced on Graham and asked him what sort of film he would like to watch. He could offer 'close-ups' for such and such a price, and so on . . .

Graham remonstrated with him, and we started to walk up

the rue de Douai. By that time, it had begun to dawn on us that we were in a red-light district teeming with brothels.

At a certain point, we stopped. Graham opened a door, and we found ourselves in a large, gloomy, dimly lit room. There was an enormous bar, behind which stood a red-headed woman who was made up to the hilt, a real caricature of a *madame de bordel.*

As soon as she set eyes on Graham, she gave a broad smile and exclaimed, 'Ah, Monsieur Greene! It's a long time since we've seen you. How are you?'

My heart sank, but Emmy was thrilled. Sitting at a table in one corner of the room I noticed a Chinese man who was absolutely sodden with alcohol or drugs and who was staring at us with dead, expressionless eyes. Shortly afterwards, the woman disappeared with Graham through a door behind the bar. There we were, left on our own, when all of a sudden I felt a hand on my shoulder. I looked round and saw the horrid face of the Chinese man. That was the last straw. I had had enough. I told Emmy I wanted to go, and I got up and left.

She followed me out into the street, protesting furiously, 'This is so stupid of you, Yvonne. For once, we had the opportunity to see something really special, and then you go and wreck all the plans Graham made for us.'

I was crying when Graham joined us outside in the street. Because it was dark, he didn't at first notice how upset I was, and he told us that everything was arranged, but that we would have to wait for an hour or so until the police had carried out their inspection.

'Shall we go for a drink somewhere nearby in the meantime?' he asked me. I didn't reply, and it was then that he realised everything had turned sour. He didn't say anything; he just hailed a passing taxi. We deposited poor, disappointed Emmy at her front door and returned to the St James and Albany. We didn't sleep much that night . . .

Next morning, Graham had an 8.30 appointment at the hotel

with Jean Anouilh to discuss plans to dramatise André Malraux's novel *La Condition humaine* for the stage. The play never materialised.

Soizic: Why did you react so violently in the rue de Douai, Yvonne? In retrospect, don't you think you behaved like a naive young thing?

Yvonne: It was because it came as such a surprise. It would never have occurred to me that he could have entertained such an idea. That sort of thing was not my cup of tea, anyway. The real problem was that I suddenly began to associate him with that dirty, shabby side of life. And yes, I was shocked, I admit. Remember, Soizic, that only a month or so earlier, we had spent a romantic evening together at La Réserve in Beaulieu. The contrast was brutal in the extreme, and I felt very badly let down. The statue had truly fallen off its pedestal. The incident didn't last long, however, and it was of no relevance or consequence as far as our relationship was concerned. Nevertheless, as a result of this Graham never made any attempt to repeat the experience, even if he did continue mentioning brothels in some of his later books, but at least his interest then was fictional!

Soizic: Was he a perfect angel in any other respect?

Yvonne: Of course not, but as far as I am concerned, he was an angel . . .

4

Burning the Boats

Soizic: During those early years of your relationship with Graham, were you not intrigued, or in due course put off, by someone who might increasingly have seemed a very strange character?

Yvonne: I was certainly intrigued, but that aroused my curiosity and spurred me to forge ahead.

Soizic: Do you mean that he had trapped you and lured you into what you have just called his 'dirty' world?

Yvonne: Not in the least. I have never been attracted to those kinds of capers. But retrospectively, in another way, I believe these whims of his stimulated me. I wanted to discover more about him. As you can see, I was far from being discouraged. What is more, I was probably too much in love with him already not to forgive him for a few little misdemeanours which very soon struck me as being insignificant.

Soizic: So what was important for you at that period?

Yvonne: In the early sixties, my main preoccupation was organising my new life in France with my two children, for whom I bore full responsibility from then on. We already had a house at Juan-les-Pins, where my father lived. That made my task easier.

Graham, for his part, still lived in England and used to shuttle back and forth between London and Nice airport. He used to stay at the Hotel Royal in Antibes at that time, on the sea-front. You only had to cross the road leading to Cap d'Antibes to swim on the Ilette beach, which belonged to the hotel. Since his trips to the south of France were becoming more and more frequent and prolonged, in 1964 he decided to rent a small flat on the sixth floor of the Floride, opposite the Albert I gardens, near the sea-wall at Antibes. In fact it was a rather modestly furnished studio flat, but to us it was home. Graham actually referred to it as 'the nest'. Those were wild, crazy years. We allowed ourselves to be carried away by passion, without worrying about the future at all. Only one thing mattered to us: to preserve our love, come what may.

Gradually, Graham emerged from his nightmare. Liberated from Querry and his doomed soul by the publication of *A Burnt-Out Case* in 1961, he could henceforth devote himself to writing *May We Borrow Your Husband?* (1967) and other stories in a much lighter vein.

The year 1966 was a turning point for him, a year of crucial decisions, both in his private life and in his work.

In November 1965 he wrote to me from London, 'Today I have been cleaning drawers, destroying letters, preparing for the new life.' Then later, on 17 December, 'Think of me on December 31, giving a farewell dinner at the Connaught to Max and Joan, the Sutros and Miss Reid.* Then, next day, I take the train at 10.00 a.m. and arrive at the Gare du Nord at 6.15 – a free man!'

Soizic: 'A free man'? What did he mean by that?

* Max Reinhardt, managing director of The Bodley Head, and his wife Joan were close friends, as were John and Gillian Sutro. Josephine Reid was Graham's secretary for many years.

Yvonne: Beyond any shadow of doubt, he was expressing a feeling of deliverance. On one hand, these constant comings and goings between England and France were beginning to exhaust him, and our separations were becoming increasingly painful. On the other, he was well aware of the consequences of such an upheaval for him and those close to him. But his determination to throw off the weight of the past would carry him through, and that was what gave him this feeling of liberation expressed in the words 'a free man'. And, as if to convince himself thoroughly of this, he said to me one day with undisguised satisfaction, 'As a symbol of my new freedom, I have decided to abandon the lined variety of paper I used to write on, where the lines seem to me now like the bars on a prison window.' A somewhat childish reflection, on the face of it, but one which said a great deal as far as he was concerned.

He had informed me about his decision to leave England and to settle permanently in France a few weeks beforehand. I scarcely dared believe it and on no account did I wish to influence him, but he had made up his mind and nothing would prevent him. It was certainly the greatest proof of his love that he could give me. I was fully aware of the magnitude of what he had done, and it filled me with joy and happiness, although my feelings were mingled with a certain anxiety as to his future and the possible repercussions for his work. But my anxiety quickly dissolved when, after a brief stay in Paris, he arrived at Nice airport looking happy and resolute.

Very soon afterwards, he acquired a comfortable, if fairly modest, two-room flat at the Résidence des Fleurs, near the harbour built by Vauban and opposite the Fort Carré, with a view of the old town on one side and the mountains on the other. He was to remain there until the end of his life. He had found his 'home' in the old town of Antibes, which he had known for ages and which he loved.

He wrote about this period, which unquestionably marked a turning-point in his life, in *Ways of Escape*:

What swung me out of the depression into the manic condition in which I wrote most of the stories in *May We Borrow Your Husband?* and then started work on *Travels with My Aunt*? I can only suppose it came from making a difficult decision in my private life and leaving England to settle permanently in France in 1966. I burned a number of boats and in the light of the flames I began again to write a novel.

It was actually in the euphoria of this time, when he was rediscovering his taste for life, that he told me one day about his intention of writing a 'serious' book on the theme of death. The book was to be called *The Last Decade*.

The first pages had been written when, in an about-turn typical of him, he decided to abandon the project, saying, 'What I am doing is absurd. I now realise that the only way of dealing with death is to treat the subject as absurd and to make fun of it.' *Travels with My Aunt* had been completed – the only one of his books, on his own admission, that he wrote for pleasure ('for the fun of it', he would have said).

Travels with My Aunt was published in 1969 to a mixed welcome, and certain reviewers were even quite harsh, particularly in Britain. He was deeply disappointed. 'My fellow countrymen won't allow me to be funny,' he told me. 'It goes against their preconceptions, what they expect of me. It doesn't tally with the label they've pinned to me. There's nothing I can do about it apart from reminding them that the subject of the book is death. It's a farce, but farce, unlike comedy, is not a cheerful genre, even if it contains some amusing scenes. The clown makes us laugh, but he himself is sad' (*Carnet rouge*).

Soizic: This book is dedicated to a mysterious 'H. H. K.'. It reads as follows: 'For H. H. K., who helped me more than I can tell', and, in your copy, Graham has added by hand, 'and for Yvonne with love from Graham'. Who is H. H. K.?

Yvonne: The initials H. H. K. stand for 'Healthy, Happy Kitten', a nickname which Alexander Stuart Frere* coined for me once when we were all bantering together among friends. I used to call him *'mon petit frère'*. Graham wanted to dedicate the book to me but for reasons of tact he adopted the initials at Frere's suggestion, even though he himself never called me by that name.

Soizic: People have gone on at great length about this period in Graham Greene's life, everyone giving their own version of facts which you throw new light on. But can you confirm that he never regretted having taken a decision of such magnitude?

Yvonne: Absolutely. And I often asked him the same question. Not only did he never regret it, but he never regarded himself as an exile living in France.

To understand this kind of behaviour, you need to know that Graham was a man who had no roots and that his real roots lay in not having any. Remember his words 'My roots are in rootlessness.'

Soizic: But didn't he consider you his roots?

Yvonne: Perhaps . . . maybe . . . Only he could have answered you and he did, in fact, provide a sort of reply to the questions that certain people asked him on this subject: it occurred at Moscow University in an interview he gave in February 1987:†

---

* A. S. Frere joined the publishing firm of William Heinemann in 1923. He was its managing director from 1932 to 1940, chairman from 1945 to 1961, and president from 1961 to 1962. His enduring friendship with Graham Greene is well known. He died on 3 October 1984, aged ninety-one.

† The interview was recorded on cassette in simultaneous translation by Tatiyana Kudriyavsteva, Graham Greene's Russian translator, who later transcribed the original version.

Question: Why do you live in France?
Answer: I always liked France and always thought of finishing my days there with good wines and good bread. And in 1966 there appeared a personal reason for this. I wanted to be closer to a certain person who was dear to me.

As far as I know, that was the furthest he went as far as revelations concerning his private life were concerned.

5

Finding a Modus Vivendi

Soizic: Graham made a very important decision when he settled in Antibes, a few kilometres from your home in Juan-les-Pins. What difference did this make to you?

Yvonne: A great deal, as you can imagine. First of all, it marked a turning-point in our relationship: what had initially appeared to be an affair without a future became from then on something which could endure and have a purpose. That, at least, was what I felt and what I wanted. I will even admit to you that by that stage I felt certain that for me he would be 'the last and the best; the best and the last'. But I still had to convince him. It was a long-term job . . .

Practically speaking, even if we were not living permanently under the same roof, from then on we were able to be together as much as we wished, given our respective obligations. There was no longer a distance between us.

Soizic: Then why didn't you live together openly?

Yvonne: No. At the very beginning I made a carefully considered choice: my life as a mother on the one hand, my life as a woman on the other. Which does not mean that the partition between the two was watertight. Graham was always a great help to me in resolving certain problems which inevitably arose with the children, but I thought it best to spare him their physical presence, which I knew would have been incompatible with his work as a writer. He needed a great deal of silence and concentration in order to write.

Soizic: So it was a deliberate choice on your part?

Yvonne: Yes, probably. Or perhaps it was cowardice . . . In 1966, when Graham made his decision to come and settle in Antibes, Martine and Brigitte were fifteen and eleven respectively; they knew nothing about my private life. I admit quite candidly that I hadn't the courage to tell them the truth because it might have risked unsettling them.

Soizic: And how did Graham react to your behaviour?

Yvonne: Not only did he agree with my point of view, but he shared my feelings of responsibility which kept me from taking any further steps. What is more, in a letter dated 20 August 1964 he wrote to me, 'I want you to live with me, but I want you to live with me without regrets.' So each of us was aware that, as far as these matters were concerned, hurried or rash decisions might be disastrous. We did not want to take any risks.

Soizic: Nevertheless, it is astonishing that such a situation should have lasted so long. To reach such decisions and keep to them, despite the pressure of the realities of everyday life. Can you explain that?

Yvonne: I find it a hard question to answer, because at the time everything seemed quite obvious to me; rather like an enormous jigsaw puzzle in which every piece slots automatically into place.

Looking back, however, perhaps it's easier for me to provide an answer of sorts. The first explanation that comes to mind has to do partly with our circumstances and partly with our different personalities.

First, the circumstances: the fact that Jacques, who had to remain in Africa because of his job,* was absent for ten months of the year, gave us the space and freedom to organise our life together in France. As for Graham, his life was prescribed by the demands of his work as a writer, which, for him in particular, had always necessitated travelling and spending time abroad: during those years, his main areas of interest were Cuba, Haiti and, later, Panama, Nicaragua and El Salvador, all countries which he refused to take me to because, he used to say, they were too dangerous. Of course, he chose the two months when I was busy with my family responsibilities to make most of those journeys (actually, he was never away for more than two weeks at a stretch, and we would arrange to meet in Antibes, London, Paris or elsewhere, and in that way interrupt our separation. 'Make a break,' as he used to say).

Furthermore, those two months during the summer (in his letters Graham occasionally described what, for him, was their frustrating aspect) allowed my daughters to be with their parents. It helped give them the illusion of normal family life a little; they believed in it and benefited greatly from it.

As far as each of our personalities was concerned, I would say that neither Graham not Jacques – for totally different reasons – was made for married life. As for me, I've always been an independent character and I don't put up easily with being tied down, for whatever reason. Each of them was intelligent enough to understand this, and they had the generosity of spirit to accept it.

Soizic: You have indeed provided the beginnings of a reply to questions one might have concerning a rather unconventional

* Jacques had a long and successful career in Africa, where he worked for a large Anglo-Dutch import and export company, UAC (United Africa Company Ltd), which had offices all along the coast of West Africa.

situation. But I still find there are too many shadowy areas. You certainly managed to find a modus vivendi which apparently satisfied you, but at what price? Was it actually as easy as your remarks make it sound? Knowing a little about the complex and tortured side of Graham's character and the stormy episodes of his earlier life, your path suddenly strikes me as being amazingly smooth and uncomplicated . . .

Yvonne: No, you certainly couldn't describe a situation which you quite correctly call 'unconventional' as 'one long, peaceful stream'. To begin with, it was hard to strike a happy balance and Graham was frequently very worried. Something he said comes to mind: 'If, one day, you no longer wanted me, and if you were to fall in love with someone else, simply send me a plain sheet of paper in an envelope; I would understand and I promise you I wouldn't pester you.'

For me, every time he went away was a wrench. Would it be a temporary absence, or would it be for ever? I could never be sure. Obviously, in a situation such as ours everything depended on mutual trust in our love for each other.

Soizic: In this complicated scenario, did the notion of divorce ever arise?

Yvonne: Yes, of course. We knew that an explosion could occur at any time. We were conscious of the risks, but ready to take them. I was not worried about the future. I knew Graham was ready to behave in a responsible way: he had taken the lessons of the past to heart in this respect, and he had adopted a cautious attitude to the subject from the early days of our relationship, saying: 'I won't try and get you involved in a divorce. Only you will decide in this matter. But I want you to know' – I can hear him saying this – 'that any time you decide to change your life you will be welcome by my side.'

Soizic: What do you mean by 'the lessons of the past'?

Yvonne: By that I understand – and I base what I say on what he himself told me – that he had learnt through experience how pointless and dangerous it is to persist in trying to make a married woman divorce her husband, particularly one who is the mother of a family. He had come to realise that such behaviour could only poison the relationship between a couple and eventually lead to the ruin of their love for each other. He was determined, therefore, not to make the same mistakes.

Soizic: But however 'reasonable' this situation may have been, it must have entailed risks, surely?

Yvonne: Any relationship between two people entails risks. Only the innocent are free of them in this respect. But I don't believe for a moment that the marriage bond constitutes a guarantee of stability for a couple. You have only to look around you to be convinced of that. All that matters, in my view, is the determination and the desire to remain together. Both of us had that determination.

So the only way my marriage could have been ended was through Jacques, who might have wished to start a new life and ask for a divorce. Naturally, we had both envisaged such an eventuality and we were prepared to confront it, as Graham made clear in a letter dated 20 August 1964: 'But if the break comes earlier, I will do all I can to make you happy.'

In spite of some tense moments which led to Jacques behaving somewhat aggressively towards me, these warnings never materialised into anything.

Soizic: Nevertheless, didn't you feel a little uneasy, from a moral point of view, because of this situation?

Yvonne: No, not at all. Notions of morality and ethics are frequently nothing but pure hypocrisy. I consider that no one has the right to judge anyone else. I have lived according to my conscience, and for me that is all that matters.

Soizic: But you are a Catholic. So was Graham. Wasn't this an obstacle to the notion of a divorce?

Yvonne: From a religious standpoint, because both of us had been married in church, we had no hope of our relationship being recognised by the Church. We were condemned, therefore, to living in adultery.

Soizic: I'm talking about divorce, not marriage . . .

Yvonne: At the risk of shocking many people, I would even say that our relationship, such as it was, being on the fringes of Christian morality, did not trouble us.

Soizic: And Graham, who was a 'better' Catholic than you and who went to mass every Sunday, what was his position?

Yvonne: It's true, he did go to mass every Sunday, which proves that he did not feel excluded from the Church and from a community to which he was pleased to belong.
On the other hand, he did not see how the fact of making love to a woman – with her consent, of course, and thereby making her happy – could be an offence towards God, which is how the sin is actually defined. So from that point of view his conscience was squared.

Soizic: And if you were to start your lives again?

Yvonne: Graham himself supplied the answer to your question in an inscription he wrote on the back of a photograph of himself taken in Bratislava in 1979: 'If I were to live my life again, there is only one thing I would want unchanged: meeting you, knowing you and loving you.' To which I replied on a plain sheet of paper: 'If I were to live my life again, I would do exactly the same. A love like this can only be a gift from God, and He could not disagree with it without disavowing Himself.'

Soizic: So no regrets, no remorse?

Yvonne: In so far as I can congratulate myself today for having retained the full affection not just of my own children but of Graham, too, I believe that we did choose the right path. What's more, we experienced only the good aspects of life, protected from all material considerations and, especially, from the habits that can kill love. I have one deep and sincere regret, however: not to have appreciated the serious nature of the illness from which Graham suffered at the end of his life, and not to have taken the decision to drop everything and be at his side, devoting myself entirely to him, until a year before his death.

6

Looking Back

Soizic: Graham Greene was very sparing in what he confided about his private life as an adult. Yet he spoke freely enough about his childhood and his adolescence. In *The Other Man*, for example, he described the 'state of happiness' of his early years surrounded by his brothers and sisters in the midst of his large family at Berkhamsted. In his autobiography, *A Sort of Life*, the perspective is more specific, but also different: behind the blissful happiness, and alongside his earliest memories, looms the knowledge of death: 'The first thing I remember is sitting in a pram at the top of a hill with a dead dog lying at my feet.'

Shortly afterwards, here as elsewhere, he recalls the feelings of failure and dread, linked to the 'boredom' that swelled inside his head like a 'balloon'. There follow, too, the revelations about 'the horror of promiscuity'* and humiliations at school; the feeling of betrayal and the 'divided loyalties' that are at the heart of Greene's work as a writer. Illuminating these states of conscience, which are diffused like beams from projectors, there are the episodes of Russian roulette, the fascination with 'the dangerous edge of things' and his undiminished attraction to the 'ways of escape'; and, ever since childhood, there was his taste for the secretive, if not for dissembling (not letting his mother know he could read, for example, or, literally, going into hiding).

* See *The Other Man*.

'In the lost boyhood of Judas/Christ was betrayed', Greene recalled, quoting A.E.'s poem 'Germinal', in order to stress what he considered to be the vital importance of childhood. But did he often talk about his own childhood with you?

Yvonne: Yes, frequently. Just as he used to ask me about my own childhood – particularly, as it happens, at the time when he was writing *A Sort of Life*. He took great pleasure in remembering the quiet, cosy atmosphere of the nursery, where time slipped slowly by in a closed, protected world which he did not leave until he was thirteen. He often used to recall the hours he spent reading to his brother Hugh, who was six years younger than him and had problems with his eyes. The only thing he could remember bothering him was the tears of 'Baby Hugh', as he referred to his brother, for he slept in the next room and sometimes woke him up at night. He would then spend time comforting him. Perhaps this helped kindle the affectionate relationship between the two men that lasted throughout their lives. He also described the joy he felt when, in the late afternoon, the magical moment arrived when his mother came to read to her children.

In this family reading was of the greatest importance. Graham had devoured the adventure stories of Marjorie Bowen, Rider Haggard and Stevenson. He also adored Beatrix Potter, whose illustrations he always admired – he kept one in his library.

Soizic: It must have been a very different childhood from your own.

Yvonne: Certainly, but how could one imagine it to have been otherwise? At home we had no nursery, there was no domestic staff, and we did not even have any paternal authority, for my father went away to make his career in Africa the year I was born. We were three children, a boy and two girls, of whom I was the youngest. My mother was a stationmaster – an unusual occupation for a woman at that time – and furthermore she took full responsibility for the family. We were very close to her; she loved us dearly and we loved her in return.

In spite of the difficulties, I remember my childhood as being full of *joie de vivre* and great freedom. Reading was not my favourite occupation. As far as I was concerned, adventure was not found in books. Adventure for me meant setting out to sea, between the ages of eight and twelve, with the local fishermen from the Crozon peninsula, where we lived. They were all chums of mine. I was Vovonne, their little shipmate, their mascot, in a way.

Soizic: So can one conclude that, all in all, Graham, like you, enjoyed a happy childhood?

Yvonne: Yes, but everything collapsed for me when, at the age of twelve, I was sent as a boarder to the *lycée* at Quimper, where I had to pass through a large pale-oak door – the door to hell or to heaven, depending on which direction you were heading. In Graham's case, he had to confront the 'green baize door' that divided the family home from the boarding-school, and the famous nursery landing where he was frightened to venture because there was a witch lurking there. Those were intense experiences for both of us.

Soizic: Weren't they somewhat exaggerated?

Yvonne: No. I spent entire nights crying. I could not bear to be separated from my mother, whose bed I used to share, my father being away most of the time. When I told him about this, Graham was moved to tears. He even insisted on coming to see my 'prison' in Quimper in 1965. He wanted me to write a story about it; he thought my title for it, '*La Boîte*', was rather good. For my part, in 1963 I had been very keen to see the school at Berkhamsted, the establishment that had thrust him so brutally into a hostile, cruel world he could not accept. It was my first trip to England. For each of us those visits were pilgrimages. I had wanted to see the 'Common' and the exact place where, after he had escaped from the boarding-house – he was sixteen at the time – his sister Molly found him, worn out with exhaustion. It was after this episode, and on the advice of his elder brother Raymond, that Graham's father sent him to see a psychoanalyst.

Soizic: There were ruptures and upsets in both your childhood and his, but it seems that he was a problematic child, unlike you.

Yvonne: That's quite clear. In my case, I think I was really a fairly normal little girl, and, actually, it was not long before the wretchedness I suffered from being sent away to boarding-school disappeared, thanks to the support of a girl there who later became a great friend. For him, however, things grew steadily worse from the age of fourteen onwards. He soon found himself the butt of jokes and teasing from his young classmates. Was this because he was what we would nowadays call a gifted child, as I once suggested to him (not that he paid much attention to my remark . . .)? Or because he lisped a little? Or was it because his unusual behaviour (he didn't like sport, among other things) made him stand out from other boys – quite apart from the fact that he thought he was a traitor in the eyes of his schoolfriends (or rather as a 'Quisling's son', as he put it), owing to his position as son of the headmaster? In any case, he was more or less aware that he was not like other children.

Soizic: Can you be more specific?

Yvonne: Well, I do recall an example of what I mean, and it is linked, as it happens, with the pilgrimage to Berkhamsted that I mentioned: we had gone there with Graham's brother Hugh. After visiting the school, I expressed a wish to go and see the Common where Graham had wandered for hours and had then sat down, exhausted, by a bush. We stopped at the very place. Graham was silent; there was an expression of horror on his face and the atmosphere was heavy. Then, without a word being said, we went to the Swan, the pub on the High Street. Hugh was the first to break the silence: 'Really, Graham, I don't understand you. Our brother Raymond and I both followed the same path at school as you did. Raymond was a prefect and a brilliant scholar. As for me, I didn't do too badly, either, and I retain some excellent memories of those days: I had some good friends, and we all got on very well together.' 'Well, then, there must have been something wrong with me at that time,' Graham muttered, as if he were emerging from a nightmare from which he could not detach himself.

In fact, the cause of these torments, which became almost pathological and were to pursue him for years, could be put down to one person: Carter.

Carter was a classmate of Graham's whom he admired and loathed simultaneously. An intelligent boy, who was probably perverse and cruel, Carter found in him the ideal victim, and did his best to humiliate him almost obsessively, both mentally and physically. Graham's only support in this relentless struggle was his one friend, Watson. His real name was Wheeler, but he was called Watson in *A Sort of Life* because Wheeler was still alive.

But eventually Watson betrayed him and moved over to the enemy camp. It was too much. Graham had a nervous breakdown and escaped from a world which had become unbearable for him.

So those are the facts of the situation, as he experienced it and as he perceived it. But much more interesting, to my mind, were the repercussions of his childhood suffering on his life as an adult and on his career as a writer: all those humiliations inflicted by his 'torturer', Carter, were responsible for his adopting an attitude from which he never deviated: the defence of the weak and the oppressed (with whom he identified) against the oppressors. A feeling of revolt against injustices, whatever they might be.

A further consequence, and one which was related above all to his friend Watson's treachery, was his determination to prove to all these 'bullies' (a word he often used) that he was capable of doing something with his life. It was in fact from this period, as he has acknowledged, that his determination to become a writer stemmed – a determination based initially upon a deep desire for revenge.

Soizic: Did the desire for revenge remain with him, and, if so, how did it express itself?

Yvonne: Certainly not in concrete form, but rather through a sort of haunting presence of what he called 'the creature under a stone': if he lifted the stone of the past, there was a danger of the beast reappearing – that beast which for many years had been linked in his mind with an unfulfilled desire for revenge. Actually, it was not until 1951, when one of life's coincidences had led to his meeting Watson again in Kuala Lumpur,* that he was able to exorcise the past; standing beside him was an insignificant colonial civil servant who came out with the remark: 'We were at school together, don't you remember? We used to go around with a chap called Carter. The three of us. Why, you used to help me and Carter with our Latin prep . . .'

As for his determination for revenge, I remember Graham saying to me one day, 'Without Carter and Watson I would probably never have become a writer.'

There was certainly a degree of reality about all the suffering he endured at Berkhamsted (Carter often used to prick him with the point of his compass, for example), but above all it was the result of his hypersensitivity and an over-endowed imagination which could not yet find its outlet in creativity, for as Graham once confessed to me on the subject of the torment he had gone through, 'I wrote it out of me.'

Soizic: I am not quite convinced he really 'wrote it out' of him. All these things affected him throughout his life, and the consequences can be found in books such as *England Made Me* (1935), *Brighton Rock* (1938), *The Lawless Roads* (1939), *The Confidential Agent* (1939), *The Ministry of Fear* (1943), his essay 'The Lost Childhood' and, of course, in *The Captain and the Enemy* (1988).

---

* The incident is recounted in *The Revenge*, one of a series of booklets specially printed by Max Reinhardt at The Bodley Head for friends of the firm. See also *A Sort of Life*, Ch. 3, part 2.

Yvonne: You're right. As a matter of fact, on 20 July 1988 he presented me with a copy of what was to be his last work of fiction, *The Captain and the Enemy*. After reading it, I asked him, 'Is the character of the twelve-year-old Victor (also Baxter III and Jim, who is also an outcast at school) based on you at Berkhamsted?'

'Yes, definitely,' was his answer.

'Did you really feel like an "Amalekite"?' I asked.*

'Yes, certainly, and even worse, if possible.'

The wounds had not healed properly yet, and never did, in fact. He couldn't find a word strong enough to describe the ordeal he underwent there.

Soizic: But before he started writing, how did he escape from the nightmare?

Yvonne: His six months in London with his psychoanalyst must certainly have helped him a great deal. From then on his torments became 'endurable', but his deep unease, his 'spleen', as he put it, still gnawed away at him. How was he to break loose? In the autumn of 1923, the discovery of a revolver in a corner-cupboard in his elder brother Raymond's bedroom seemed to provide a temporary solution.† This was the 'Russian roulette' episode.

Soizic: Did he talk about this with you?

Yvonne: Rarely. He seemed ill at ease when the subject arose. The only aspect he truly regretted was to have discussed it with other people; for he soon realised that his name could not be mentioned without it being associated with Russian roulette. It saddened him.

* The Amalekites were a wandering tribe in the south Negev Desert, who were exterminated by the Hebrews in the days of Saul and David.

† In *Journey without Maps* he described his experiences during a night of terror: 'I had always assumed before, as a matter of course, that death was desirable.' See also *Ways of Escape* (London: The Bodley Head, 1980), p. 54.

The only time Graham was amused by the subject was in 1983, during a meeting with Fidel Castro and Gabriel García Márquez in Cuba. When he returned from this trip to Latin America and Cuba, he gave me, as usual, an account of his journey: 'The subject of Russian roulette came back to haunt me, introduced by Gabo [García Márquez]. Fidel asked me whether it was true. I said, "Yes it is." Then he exclaimed, "But you shouldn't be alive." '* And after that they went on to discuss the mathematical risks Graham had taken. The funny side of that discussion with Fidel still made him laugh.

Soizic: In your opinion, did he really want to commit suicide?

Yvonne: I've asked myself that question, of course. He certainly took great risks, but he also confessed to me one day: 'I never thought it would work.'

Paradoxical though this may seem, death was not the aim of his action; it was something which can only be explained by his desperate need for a strong surge of emotion in order to escape momentarily from the melancholia he was suffering.

Soizic: Was he capable of suicide?

Yvonne: In my view, he was not the sort of person to commit suicide. The only proof I can offer is his reaction when, in the depths of Liberia, he really did come within a hair's breadth of death, something he recalled a propos *Journey without Maps*. About that nightmarish experience of being very sick with fever, he wrote, 'I had always assumed before, as a matter of course, that death was desirable. It seemed that night an important discovery. It was like a conversion . . . I had been completely convinced of the beauty and desirability of the mere act of living.'†

---

* Graham also referred to this in *Getting to Know the General*, 1983.
† *Ways of Escape*, p. 54.

7

'But who are you, Mr Greene?'

Soizic: Graham Greene was always prepared to talk about his books, but the moment his private life was mentioned the door closed: you could pry no further. But who was he really?

Yvonne: Most interviews with journalists actually ended with the question 'But who are you, Mr Greene?' His reply shot out, laconic and final: 'I am my books.' It was pointless persisting, and they left feeling frustrated.

I confess that I had difficulty understanding this myself to begin with, for whenever he spoke about himself, as you must have noticed, he always used the word 'one', never 'I', even when it concerned the mildest things, and I sometimes used to wonder who it was who was hiding behind this anonymous 'one', before I came to realise that he was speaking about himself.

Later on, when I told him about the problems I had with the word, he stopped using it.

That discreet silence of his obviously gave free rein to all sorts of hypotheses and interpretations as to his true personality.

I certainly cannot pretend to have known him completely, but perhaps it may be possible to lift the veil slightly over the complex and mysterious personality that was Graham Greene.

Soizic: Was he as 'complex' and 'mysterious' as all that, in your opinion?

Yvonne: There can be no doubt that he was complex: he was an unpredictable human being, who was in constant conflict with himself and who was torn apart by violent urges. He was a cyclothymiac, who switched abruptly from euphoria to depression. But in my view that was part of his charm, and it is astonishing to think that a man who suffered so much within himself from boredom should never have been considered boring by others. People often called him 'the hunted man', but he was only ever hunted by himself, a victim of the traps that, unconsciously or not, he had set up around himself.

He was someone who was plagued by impulses which were sometimes irrational and often contradictory. These contradictions were in keeping with his emotions: that is to say, they were extreme, and when he returned to reality, he would curse himself.

Was he mysterious? For me, the real mystery of Graham Greene lay in the power and variety of his creative imagination. Occasionally, I used to take his head in my hands and say to him, 'How do you manage to imagine all this and create all these characters in this head of yours?' And he replied, 'They don't come from there; they come from my bowels.' We burst out laughing and the mystery remained. It was not a time for serious discussion.

Soizic: Aren't you frightened of destroying the image of himself that he sought to create? Did he want to create an image of himself?

Yvonne: He never wanted to create an image. It was simply that he loathed talking about himself in public. That's what he meant when he said, 'Whenever I talk about myself, I wear a mask.'

His reticence can easily be understood when you realise that he was a shy man – as you know – and, furthermore, someone who did not like himself: 'There's another man within me that's angry with me' (Sir Thomas Browne; used as epigraph to *The Man Within*). Conversely, he was perfectly aware of all his weaknesses but, out of modesty and pride, he preferred to keep them to himself in the main and not say anything which might reveal them to the public. So he was constantly on his guard.

Soizic: Was there a great difference between his public life and his private life?

Yvonne: I wouldn't use the terms 'public life' and 'private life'. But certainly his behaviour changed when he felt at ease among friends or, *a fortiori*, with the woman he loved: the shy, secretive man then became very open, talkative and full of energy.

All in all, he acted a role in public. In private, he was natural; he was himself.

Soizic: So why did he conceal his private life so much?

Yvonne: For obvious reasons of decency, since our life together did not conform to normal standards or conventions. Also out of respect for the pride and feelings of those who were close to us.

In any case, discretion had always been our watchword from the very beginning. We had both learnt from experience how dangerous it is to allow people to interfere in a couple's relationship. It's a poison that kills. But that did not prevent us from leading a 'normal' life and in no way did it imply a new version of *Back Street*.*

Soizic: Was his refusal to appear on television – he only once agreed to be filmed and that was in the Soviet Union; on the other two occasions he was filmed without his knowledge – to do with protecting his privacy?

* A 1941 comedy by Robert Stephenson, adapted from a novel by Fanny Hurst, in which a married man has a relationship with his mistress for over thirty years.

Yvonne: It so happens that I once asked him that very question. This is what he said: 'I refuse for various reasons. Mainly, because I believe a writer is not a public figure. His books may be well known – that's only to be desired – but he himself should remain anonymous.

'Next, because television is a formidable weapon. If you're successful, you allow yourself to be lured irresistibly, and then the actor takes over from the writer. That's what happened notably to Malcolm Muggeridge in England. And if the appearance isn't going to be a success . . . why do it?

'It's a decision I took from the very beginning as far as British television is concerned, and it wouldn't be fair to change now. Those who approached me in the past would be resentful' (*Carnet rouge*).

Another reason came to light during lunch one day at Chez Félix in the port of Antibes with Graham's doctor and friend, Georges Rosanoff, and his wife, Mona. Georges asked, 'Why is it, Graham, that we never see you on television? Is it out of modesty?' Graham replied, 'No, Georges, out of pride.'

A little later on, when I asked him for an explanation, he answered, 'It's a publisher's job to obtain publicity for a book on television. Not the author's' (*Carnet rouge*).

Of course, this attitude could always be interpreted as a subterfuge, but personally I doubt it. The true reason for his determination to preserve his anonymity was that it was essential to him in his profession: to be able to observe people in their natural state, without masks, and without feeling that they were being watched.

The subject often came up in our conversations, whether in private or among friends. I remember, for example, a lunch party with Charlie and Oona Chaplin, and Max and Joan Reinhardt, at Chez Germaine in the harbour at Villefranche-sur-Mer. We had scarcely sat down at table when a horde of journalists fell upon Charlie and snapped away at him with their cameras before at last leaving us alone. Charlie then asked,

'Why is it, Graham, that they all want to photograph me and not you?' Graham replied, 'But it's quite normal, Charlie. You, you're a public personality. I'm not one and I don't ever want to be.'

How should we interpret this exchange? Are we to conclude that Graham Greene had more to hide about himself and his private life than Charlie Chaplin did? I doubt it, but neither do I believe that either of them could exactly be called 'very humdrum', as the French writer Gérard Guégan once described Graham in an affectionate way.

Soizic: Nevertheless, I wonder what part mystification or mischievousness played in his maintaining the mystery?

Yvonne: It wasn't either of those two elements, and perhaps we should try to clarify that apparently anodyne remark 'I am my books', which left everyone free to imagine the man as being like his characters. For although none of them resembles him completely, it is clear that there is an aspect of his own character in each one of them. Here we touch on the whole problem of autobiographical elements in fiction, which I'm sure we shall return to. But was he really aware of this himself? One day I put the following question to him: 'You've often been identified with such and such a character from your books. What's your view of this?' His answer, which I jotted down in my red notebook (my *Carnet rouge*), was as follows: 'None of my characters is really like me. But there is always something in their character, or in the feelings they experience, which comes from me. Otherwise, how could I describe them? And then it's possible that one particular character may resemble me more than another: Daintry, perhaps, in *The Human Factor*, to name just one.'*

Much later, rereading this passage in my notebook, Graham

* This took place in 1978. *The Human Factor* had just been published. My question was solely to do with the characters in this book, even if I did not make that clear in the way I asked the question.

wrote in the margin, 'Daintry: I'm surprised that I identified this character with myself, even though he inhabited my former apartment in St James's Street. I thought I had physically based him on a character I knew during my first months in the Secret Service, a man who, unlike me, would have been quite at home at a shooting weekend.'

As we can see, therefore, the margin between the conscious and the subconscious is a narrow one, but perhaps it is here that we discover the validity of his comment 'I am my books'.

This reticence in talking about himself went far beyond mystification or mischievousness, which he couldn't care less about. What mattered to him was not betraying his 'inner self' to the public, not revealing that instinct of the artist which, although it took no account of the man himself, was the source of his inspiration and creativity.

All the same, one should avoid confusing Graham Greene's life with his fiction, as Norman Sherry has not hesitated to do, and, still more, avoid inventing myths. I am thinking in particular of Michael Shelden's biography *Graham Greene: The Man Within*,* which in my opinion is nothing but a grotesque and obscene mockery.

Soizic: What is it about this book that strikes you as so shocking?

Yvonne: What shocks me deeply is the spirit of the text itself, which makes it clear that the author's intentions were malicious and that he was determined to portray his subject as a monster. From start to finish everything was cleverly calculated and invented with that aim in view.

For example, Michael Shelden states that Graham Greene was homosexual and as proof reveals that Graham owned a teddy-bear which he took with him everywhere in his suitcase –

* Title of British edition, published by Heinemann in 1994.

this teddy-bear being, according to Shelden, a symbol of homosexuality . . .

In actual fact, the teddy-bear had been given to him by A. S. Frere's son, 'Tob', who possessed an ancient one-eyed threadbare teddy which had survived a shipwreck in which Frere almost lost his life. Frere was convinced that it was owing to the bear that he had escaped drowning, and the creature became his mascot, a wise creature who accompanied him everywhere and who at night, when he was asleep, gave him good advice. When Graham heard this touching little story, he expressed his admiration and said that he was even a touch envious of his old friend 'Tob'. Then, in January 1963, when we went to stay with the Freres in Barbados for the first time, there was a present waiting for Graham: a superb little teddy-bear with a blue satin ribbon round its neck.

In a letter dated 27 July 1963, on notepaper headed Hotel Nacional, Havana, Graham told me about his bear: 'Teddy is looking out of the window now. I think he likes Havana.'

And that's how, from a simple, childish story concerning friends of long standing, Michael Shelden deliberately distorted the picture and then made use of it in order to discredit, in his own way (for it should be understood that, according to him – unlike Graham Greene, who had many homosexual friends – homosexuality is a defect), the man of genius to whom he claimed he was paying tribute.*

---

* For the record, I want to make it clear that Michael Shelden came to see me in Corseaux, in Switzerland, in August 1991, on the recommendation of Pat Frere (Edgar Wallace's daughter), a 'friend' of many years. Throughout the two hours or so that we spent together, he never stopped talking about Norman Sherry and the latter's inability to write an adequate biography of Graham Greene. I realised that a battle royal was about to break out and that, without a doubt, the victim in this struggle for glory – and for money – could only be Graham Greene, the subject of their efforts, who had died five months previously.

After that – and in spite of repeated appeals by letter or by telephone – I stubbornly refused any further discussion with him. Mr Shelden's claims concerning my participation in his biography are therefore pure lies.

But in the flood of vile insinuations, which I do not intend to discuss here, not even simply to prove how inane they are, there is one which beats all the others in its degree of aberration: it is his interpretation of the story of the horrible crime perpetrated in Brighton on 17 June 1934 and which is known as the 'Brighton Trunk Murder'. This crime has never been solved, but where all Scotland Yard's finest sleuths have failed he, Michael Shelden, sixty years later, discovered who was guilty of the murder. The culprit, as you may have guessed, was none other than Graham Greene. The proof? Greene had a dream: 'One recalled a dream in which Greene feared that the police would arrest him for murdering someone and leaving the body at the cloakroom of a railway station' (*Graham Greene: The Man Within*, p. 235).

As far as that biography is concerned, I entirely support the views of Martin Stannard in his review in the *New York Times Book Review* of 2 July 1995: 'For all the cosmetic changes, *Graham Greene: The Enemy Within** remains a calculated act of malice. It is difficult to murder a corpse, but Michael Shelden does his best.' And he concluded: ' "Biographies", as Mr Shelden himself admits, "are stories, but they do not have to be fantasies." '

Soizic: Yet Graham Greene does seem to have been disliked by quite a number of people. How do you explain that?

Yvonne: He was loved or loathed, but no one was indifferent to him. In his lifetime, he knew he was disliked by certain of his fellow writers, for the literary world, too, is merciless. He knew who his enemies were and he was quite capable of defending himself, as was the case with Anthony Burgess, for example, when after a period of mutual admiration and friendship, they began to make vicious attacks on one another through the press.

* Title of US edition, published by Random House.

But could he have imagined the extent of the hatred and aggression that was to be unleashed after his death? The question may legitimately be asked. In actual fact, about a month before his death Graham suddenly came up to me and asked: 'Do you remember a short story of mine called "The Destructors" [published in 1954]?' 'Yes, of course, especially since it was one of the series of films [*Shades of Greene*] made by Thames Television, and we helped Hugh* with the filming of the story. Why do you ask?' 'Because I don't think it was very well understood or appreciated by the public. In my view it is a good story. But the tide changes and, who knows, one day, it might be revived. I won't see it. But you will.'

At the time I didn't pay very much attention to this conversation, but during the summer of 1994, when I was feeling shattered by the campaign of denigration against him, I was reminded of it and I reread the story.

'The Destructors' is about a house in the eastern suburbs of London which has suffered bomb damage during the war. A group of young louts do their best to destroy completely a house owned by an old man. While the owner is away, they manage to wreck the house, but the man survives the determined efforts of the 'destructors'. The old man is known as 'Old Misery'. His real name is Mr Thomas. (Thomas also happened to be the name chosen by Graham at his baptism when he was converted to Catholicism.) It really was a strange coincidence. Once again, was it a premonition of what was to happen after his death? It wouldn't surprise me. But I also see it as a symbol for the future: Old Misery surviving his destroyers. Could one imagine a sweeter revenge?

---

* Graham's brother, Hugh, later Sir Hugh Greene, director-general of the BBC, 1960–69. Hugh was an adviser on the series.

8

Getting Closer to the Man

Soizic: It's clear that Graham Greene was a tormented and enigmatic character, a man who was reserved, if not cold, in public: the 'grim' Greene. But he was also the genial and relaxed man his friends knew. The portraits that writers have drawn of him mirror this duality and these paradoxes at a deeper level: 'Laughter in the shadow of the gallows', according to a Swedish critic; 'an archbishop or a murderer', in the words of Paul Theroux, referring to his physical appearance. 'I'm constantly being told that I have only two masks: Boredom and Amusement,' Greene remarked sarcastically to me one day when, feeling a little apprehensive and disconcerted, I confessed to him that I had never seen 'a man change faces so often without "batting an eyelid" '.*

The physical aspect of the man – that tall, nonchalant figure, slightly stooped and with his back already slightly bent; those blue, timeless, almost vitreous eyes, which looked through and beyond you – has also added substance to the mystery of the man and his literary genius. The effect he produced could be summed up in one word: awe. That's what one felt in his presence.

But what effect did Graham Greene have on you, Yvonne? How did you react to the flesh-and-blood Graham you knew?

* See *The Other Man: Conversations with Graham Greene*, p. 24.

Did your attitude alter over the period that you knew him? And, first and foremost, can you really remember what you felt?

Yvonne: My life with Graham Greene is inscribed in my memory just as it would be in a book. I can remember everything down to the smallest detail. I've already mentioned our first meeting at my house in Douala, with Hô Bouccarut. Naturally, I was very shy, even a bit overwhelmed, but I was far more affected by what he represented for me at the time – that is, his reputation as a writer – than by his physical appearance.

My viewpoint naturally changed as our relationship evolved and I discovered, over the course of months and later years, the multiple facets of his personality that fascinated me.

His physical appearance, which to begin with left me totally indifferent, gradually began to arouse burgeoning feelings within me, and his eyes, which initially always seemed to be gazing into space, would suddenly sparkle with flashes which said a great deal. They were the first signs of an adventure which was to lead us on a long journey.

Soizic: What are the impressions that remain strongest today?

Yvonne: Whenever I delve back into my past and into my life with Graham, one very strong feeling predominates and sums up all the others simultaneously: I believe that I was very lucky to meet him and to have been able to keep him for so long. The reality has considerably surpassed the dreams I used to have as a young girl, when, as boarders at the *lycée* in Quimper, my friends and I used to imagine 'the man of my life'. I pictured him as tall and dark, with blue eyes . . . and I wanted him to be a civil servant, a job which in my mind was synonymous with security. As for love, it was something vague and nebulous at that time, something I occasionally glimpsed in stories I heard or in books I read.

Today, with the hindsight of experience, I believe I can say I know the true meaning of the words 'to love' and 'to be loved', and I am conscious that fate has spoilt me and treated me very kindly, beyond my wildest dreams. I was spoilt by his behaviour towards me: the tenderness and solicitude he showered upon me; the thousands of tiny, attentive things he did which gave me confidence and made me feel I was indispensable to him. Whenever I did something for him or helped him resolve a problem, he used to thank me warmly and say, 'You see, what would I do without you?' I often heard him use those words.

He was a considerate man, who in our day-to-day life worried about my wellbeing – too much so, at times. Whenever I happened to be lost in silence, during a walk, for example, he would quickly intervene. 'A penny for your thoughts, please,' he used to say, a little anxiously. Whenever he escaped from himself, on the other hand, losing himself momentarily in the world of his imagination and then returning to reality again, he would ask my forgiveness, saying, 'It can't be much fun for you living with a writer; I'm there, close to you physically, but you're well aware that my mind is elsewhere. Forgive me.' I understood this so well that one day it occurred to me to say, 'Don't worry. I'll never be jealous of your books.' 'And I'll never be jealous of your children' was his reply. We were all square with one another, for his books were also his children.

Since we're talking about the impressions uppermost in my mind, I should like to tell you what I miss most cruelly today. It's his strong presence beside me, that cosy and reassuring feeling that nothing bad could ever happen to me as long as he was there to protect me. We certainly experienced some testing times together during those long years, but there were two of us to confront them, and he was so determined to overcome obstacles that he instilled strength in me, the strength to fight together, whatever the circumstances. I do feel very lost without him today, and in my turn I feel I want to paraphrase his words and say to him, 'What can I do without you?'

Soizic: Physically – if it's not tactless and you don't think I'm overstepping the mark – what was it that appealed to you particularly about him?

Yvonne: Without a moment's hesitation, I would say his skin. I've always thought that skin plays an important part in love affairs. The texture of his skin was so soft and delicate that it made you quiver with delight. It's a good approach to love, don't you think?

He wasn't at all aware of this and refused to discuss such matters, but I did manage to amuse him by telling him something that my daughter Brigitte, who was four and a half at the time, once said. It was in August 1959; we had decided to go with friends to the beach known as the Plage de Passable, at Cap Ferrat. Graham, who was staying at the Hôtel de la Voile d'Or, overlooking the harbour at Saint-Jean, had come to join us for a while; he was wearing canvas espadrilles on his feet. Brigitte, who was highly observant, had come to find me and she whispered in my ear, very discreetly: 'Mummy, did you see what beautiful skin "Gram Grim" has on the tops of his feet?' The special quality of Graham's skin had even attracted the attention of a child of four and a half . . .

I have no intention of reviewing all Graham's physical qualities or defects, but I should nevertheless like to mention the beauty of his hands at this point. They were elegant, long and aristocratic. I loved caressing them. Unfortunately, in the early 1970s they became deformed by Dupuytren's disease, which made it difficult for him to write, but even so they retained all their nobility.*

* Graham's left hand was operated on, but he refused to have an operation on his right hand, because it would have meant being unable to write for at least three months, something he would not contemplate.

Lastly, I want to mention his natural elegance, which was devoid of sophistication, but had what I would call distinction, of the kind that requires no artifice. Elegant clothing, however, was the least of his worries. At the end of 1965, before he left England, he had two tweed jackets and two pairs of corduroy trousers made for him, the two outfits being absolutely identical. For town wear, he had two suits, both grey, with thin, light grey stripes, and both identical as well. His only luxury was his ivory silk shirts, which he ordered from Malaysia. As for his ties, they were either dark green or burgundy. And he felt very comfortable dressed like that, anonymously, in uniform, and blending in with the masses, yet not deceiving anyone as to his nationality, which he was very proud of.

Soizic: Yes, one can easily imagine the discreet, modest writer, a little greyish in colour perhaps, very much the 'Grim Greene' so often described – at least, very close to that portrait, don't you think?

Yvonne: No, not at all! He may have been self-effacing in the way he dressed, but he could be quite unrestrained in his behaviour. What I mean is that he could be witty and he made jokes, he was whimsical and often did the unexpected, and he had a highly developed sense of humour. His taste for practical jokes is well known, and I remember that in England he and his friend John Sutro once founded a spurious organisation known as the Anglo-Texan Society,* which was so successful and attracted so many members, many of them from the smartest levels of society, that it was still being talked about in 1976, even though the two jolly founders had both chosen to live in the South of France.

Later on, after he had settled in France, that type of joke gradually lost some of its appeal. But I do recall an evening at

---

* The Anglo-Texan Society was conceived in a mood of tipsy frivolity by Greene and Sutro in 1953.

his flat in Paris in the mid-sixties, when we were with your parents. Your father,* who had been in the French Secret Service, and Graham, who had been in MI6 during the war, discovered that they shared this wonderful common ground and an unforeseen way of ridiculing the world of espionage. Like two schoolboys out for fun, they began dreaming up an Old Spies Club, each of them mischievously dredging up names of people and reasons for their joining the club. The notion seemed so absurd and so appealing that they began to get very excited about it, and when the time came for them to part, they promised each other that they would continue to think about their crackpot scheme, which, of course, came to nothing.

Anyway, it didn't matter, because for each of them it did provide an opportunity to cement their friendship. In Graham's case, it was rather like his participating incognito in a film by François Truffaut. That was also an occasion for the two men to get better acquainted.

Soizic: Do you mean to say the ultra-discreet Greene actually acted in a film?

Yvonne: Yes, Graham was even a film star! It was in late 1983, and François Truffaut was finishing shooting his film *La Nuit américaine* at the Victorine studios in Nice. Michael Meyer,

---

* Yves Allain (1922–66). In a letter to *The Times* of 24 November 1966, Graham Greene wrote: 'The brutal murder of Yves Allain in Morocco less than two weeks after his arrival to take up the position of Chief of Post for the O.R.T.F. Rabat will come as a shock to his many English friends. He was a man of great courage, loyalty and integrity, how much courage was shown very early, when he was hardly out of college, as one of the *grands résistants* in Brittany. He directed the famous Bourgogne escape network to which some 250 Allied airmen owed their freedom, and he personally accompanied to the Spanish border many men who spoke not a word of French. He received as his British award a modest M.B.E. like so many heroes and heroines of the Resistance; his French decorations included the Croix de Guerre with palm, the Medal of the Resistance and the Légion d'Honneur, and his American the Medal of Freedom.'

who had been a friend of Graham's since 1944, had come down to the Côte d'Azur because his girlfriend at the time, Mademoiselle X, had a part in the film. He telephoned Graham to arrange a rendezvous in Antibes, and so the four of us all met for dinner at Chez Félix, by the harbour. Naturally, we talked a lot about the film that was being shot, and then Michael told us the following anecdote: 'Truffaut's very fed up. The film is nearing completion and he still hasn't found a suitable person for the tiny part of an insurance salesman who is English but speaks French. I proposed myself for the role, but when I was presented to Truffaut I was refused. The reason: "You look too intellectual for an insurance salesman." Graham's immediate reaction was: "In that case, perhaps I'd fit the bill." We took that for a joke, but Graham insisted. After dinner, all four of us went to a villa at Cap d'Antibes rented by Jacqueline Bisset, the star of the film. A party had been organised by Truffaut and all the crew were there. Graham was introduced to Truffaut as Mr Brown. He was greeted favourably by the director, who asked his assistant to arrange a meeting at the Victorine studios. When he was summoned a few days later, Graham wore a grey-striped suit, cream shirt and bottle-green tie, and carried the indispensable umbrella, and caught the train to Nice, where a car was waiting to take him to the studios. Truffaut was very pleased with his performance, but when the time came for his assistant to disclose the hoax – in other words who Mr Brown really was – he almost fainted.

'A few days later, we all had dinner again at Chez Félix, and that's how Graham Greene came to be an insurance salesman in Truffaut's *La Nuit américaine*.'*

Soizic: Did it require special circumstances – or a certain conviviality or affinity with people – for his sense of humour and fun to emerge?

* The title of the film in English is *Day for Night*. Graham Greene's hand appeared in *The Stranger's Hand*, a film made in 1954, co-produced by Greene and directed by Mario Soldati.

Yvonne: Not particularly, no. Naturally, when he was in the company of friends he made an effort to play to the gallery, but his innate sense of humour, which often consisted of self-mockery, was spontaneous. Wearing a deadpan expression, he used to take one unawares with stories which were totally out of context. There was one he told me which I liked especially and which went like this. 'One day, I went to call on a woman friend who owned a parrot that didn't speak much. The bird was normally given the freedom of the flat or was allowed to sit on its mistress's shoulders. On this particular day, it was in its cage. I went up to it and, in order to distract it, I began imitating the cry of a sheep, in the hope that it would do the same. The bird obstinately refused to speak. I continued bleating at it: "Baaa-a-a-". Suddenly, the parrot looked me straight in the face and, with its head cocked to one side, said quite clearly, "Are you all right?" I never felt so silly in my life,' Graham admitted.

I jotted down the story in my red notebook. Sometime later, when I looked at it again, I noticed that Graham had added a further little humorous note about the parrot: after the words 'didn't speak much', he had scribbled in the margin, 'The only human thing it imitated was the drawing of a wine cork. It never, except on this occasion, used words.'

Soizic: We're actually a long way from the tormented human being we mentioned earlier!

Yvonne: It was not the least contradictory thing about him, for alongside this jovial aspect of his personality – which the general public did not know about – the tormented and melancholic side of his nature was just as real and went far deeper. It was this that provided the inspiration for a number of the characters in his books. The melancholia remained with him to the end of his life. And he knew what he was talking about when he wrote, 'Melancholy is much harder to cope with than sadness: one knows the reasons for sadness. One looks in vain for the causes of melancholy' (*Carnet rouge*).

Soizic: Was it because he couldn't find the causes of his melancholy, and because he suffered so much as a result of it, that he flirted with suicide?

Yvonne: In his case, melancholy was actually something chronic. I would go so far as to call it an illness, which had manifested itself since childhood and which had gnawed away at him remorselessly all his life.

At moments of crisis, he saw no alternative to suicide and he was prepared to take all the risks. But he imposed certain restrictions, none the less. The risks were calculated. In my view he was more of a gambler than a genuinely suicidal person. And I base what I say on hard evidence: discussing his experiences in Vietnam during the war against the French (he liked to recall his memories of that period), he confessed to me that he had been won over by the women, the sunsets and, above all, by what he called 'that feeling of exhilaration which a measure of danger brings to the visitor with a "return ticket"'.*

Much later, in 1968, a year after the Six-Day War between Israel and Egypt, when people were still being killed by mortar fire on both sides of the Suez Canal, and with each country attributing blame to the other, Graham was anxious to be on the spot to see the situation for himself. Taking enormous risks, he ventured on to the banks of the canal with Moshe Dayan's son-in-law. Machine-guns were firing from every direction and, although they were lying on the sand, his companion was wounded in the ear. On his return, Graham said to me, 'Never again. I'm too old now to be killed like this, away from home.' For a time, danger had been a stimulus to him and had dispelled

* Greene's introduction to *The Quiet American* in the collected edition of his work published by Heinemann and Bodley Head in 1973.

boredom or melancholy. He had even consciously put his life in the balance, but a last-minute reflex had, on this occasion as on all the others, rescued him from the tendency to take further risks.

Soizic: So, in your opinion, he was not the type of man to commit suicide. His instinct for survival prevailed, in the final analysis.

Yvonne: Yes, but the cycle of suffering would resume again. It was only a brief respite.

Soizic: What was it that tormented him so?

Yvonne: Mostly, it was a feeling of guilt towards those whom he had caused to suffer, because he was a responsible man and, even though he was generous to other people and always ready to forgive them, he was very harsh where he himself was concerned, shouldering full responsibility for what he called his 'past errors'.

He dragged this millstone behind him, attempting by every means possible to escape from it momentarily: hence the journeys, the need to be on the move in order that the 'ice should not melt' beneath his feet, the opium, and even that sort of mental reprieve which the anaesthetic before an operation afforded him, as happened in February 1979, when he under-went an operation for cancer of the colon. He went so far as to say, 'Before the operation, while I was being taken on a trolley, feeling rather drugged already, I had an enormous feeling of relief, of liberation: not having to feel the least responsibility either for oneself or for other people, being able to place oneself entirely in the hands of the surgeons and telling yourself that from now on nothing depends on you any longer, is a mar-vellous moment for me' (*Carnet rouge*).

Soizic: What enormous guilt that reveals . . . But what did he mean by 'past errors'?

Yvonne: He never forgave himself for having made the women he loved suffer – even his wife, Vivien. But he refused to give in to pity, which was a sentiment he despised. This is what he said to me on the subject in the course of a conversation: 'Unlike compassion, pity is a contemptible sentiment. There is an element of condescension in pity which can sometimes do great harm. With compassion, by contrast, one is dealing with people on equal terms. What I call the "Scobie complex"* is not a noble sentiment at all' (*Carnet rouge*).

And it is here, perhaps, that we come to understand 'the heart of the matter': given the choice, he preferred to abandon people rather than inflict pity.

Soizic: But then why, if he had such a strong feeling of guilt (and it's greatly to his credit), do his biographers speak of his cruelty to women?

Yvonne: One cannot deny that he had made women suffer. Some of his writings testify to it and he himself could not find sufficiently hard words to describe his own behaviour. What is more, he once admitted to you just how oppressed he felt by 'this sense of having been cruel, unjust', and he added, 'It still torments me often enough before I go to sleep.'†

For all that, can one really use the word 'cruelty'? In my opinion, there's a sort of relentlessness about real cruelty, I would even say jubilation in making others suffer.

Yet, when he talked to me about his past, an impression of panic emerged clearly from his accounts, something of the anguish of an animal caught in a trap from which it doesn't

---

* Scobie is the principal character in *The Heart of the Matter*.
† *The Other Man*, p. 20.

know how to escape. It was particularly obvious during his forties, which he often described to me as the most chaotic and troubled period of his life.

I am wary of making any judgements about Graham's past, but here again there is a paradox, in my view. Why, if he had been so 'cruel', did all the women, without exception, with whom he had shared his life choose to maintain friendly relations with him after the break-up? (I am basing what I say on verifiable facts.) Let everyone draw their own careful conclusions. A passage from Marcel Proust, I think, comes to my mind: 'This indifference to the suffering we cause and which, whatever other name we may give it, is a terrible and lasting form of cruelty.'

To bring this subject to a close, I should like to mention the particularly distressing case of Dorothy Glover, his companion during the war and until 1947, when she left London to live in the country with her old mother. Graham had helped her financially so that she could buy a small house. He assigned a pension to her, a modest one, certainly, but it helped her to make ends meet; and I can attest to the fact, because I was there, that he shed bitter tears when, in 1971, he learnt of her death in pitiful conditions. I saw Graham cry only twice during our whole life together.

9

The Job of Writing

Soizic: Clarity and simplicity are the two qualities that seem to characterise Graham Greene's style and his writing. It's a style which is so nondescript, and so hard to define or classify, that it can seem quite baffling to those who try to resolve this paradox: how can the sand that slips through one's fingers so easily also be said to be typical of Graham Greene? So much so that once, in a *New Statesman* competition for the best parody of Greene's style, the winning entry was actually by Greene himself – he had great fun, doing this on several occasions, and it seems to have been a spur to that kind of production which went on until April 1980 (*Yours etc*). The second prize was awarded to someone who knew him very well – his brother Hugh!

Those distinctive characteristics – clarity and simplicity – conceal an enormous amount of sustained and relentless hard work, as is evident from Yvonne's answers; an arduous path strewn with pitfalls, with terrifying blockages and sheer hard sweat, as well as surprises, when the creator is confronted by his characters, who have acquired an independence and motivation of their own. The driving force for all this really was an obsession; his obsession to write.

But why did he write?

Yvonne: Writing was a therapy for him, something which was vital and necessary to him and which he was perfectly well aware of when he said, 'I wonder how those who don't write, or paint, or compose music, manage to cope with life. Writing is a very painful process, but I feel infinitely more upset and depressed when I'm not writing' (*Carnet rouge*).

This obsessive urge to write tormented him until the end of his life, instilling in him a permanent dread, which is conveyed by a remark I often heard him make: 'I am afraid of living too long away from work', or again: 'Retirement is always a distressing time for a man. But for a writer it is death, for in our profession everything depends on him and not on his circumstances.'*

And he never gave in.

Soizic: Did he often talk to you spontaneously about his work?

Yvonne: In the main he replied to the questions I put to him, if I refer back to the extracts from our conversations that I kept in my *Carnet rouge*. Throughout our entire life together, I did my best to understand the very complex mechanism of writing, and I tried to unravel the mystery. Was I successful? Only partially, for there are shadowy areas which he himself could not explain and which may simply have to do with a writer's genius (a phrase that he would undoubtedly have rejected, since he once said, referring to an article that mentioned 'Greene's genius', 'I am not a genius. I am a craftsman who writes books at the cost of long and painful labour' (*Carnet rouge*)).

Anything I have to say on this matter is based solely upon what he told me and what I was able to observe.

Soizic: What stands out in all of this?

Yvonne: There are two rather different considerations I remember in particular: the suffering that writing caused him,

* Random notes made by Yvonne.

and what for me were the interesting casual conversations we had about certain technical aspects of writing.

Soizic: You have mentioned 'suffering' once again. Can one ever escape from this notion when discussing Graham Greene?

Yvonne: I would say that in this case it was a question of 'positive' suffering. He once said, 'The development of a book is a bit like the gestation period of a child; but in the first instance the pregnancy is always long and painful' (*Carnet rouge*). The suffering was physical and real enough. I only had to see him after he had completed his day's work, with his pale face, his drawn features and his eyes reddened by exhaustion, to understand the level of concentration to which he subjected himself. To such an extent that one day, puzzled by these exterior signs of fatigue, I asked, 'What is it that seems particularly difficult to you – the most difficult and the most important thing – about a novel?' This was his reply: 'Everything is difficult and everything is important, but the trickiest part, in my opinion, is creating characters, and making them real and alive. At the outset, a character is nothing but a tiny speck, a speck which I concentrate upon with such intensity that after two or three hours my eyes begin to water and I am obliged to stop. Then this speck grows bigger, looms closer, and gradually – very slowly – takes shape. Then, if everything proceeds smoothly, he becomes alive and even independent; he acquires his own character and his own will, outside and independent of me. In *The Human Factor*, for example, when I started to write the scene in the confessional between Castle and the priest, I did not have the following passage in mind for a moment: "The priest looked reluctantly round. His eyes were bloodshot. Castle had an impression that he had fallen by a grim coincidence on another victim of loneliness and silence like himself." It was Castle himself who wanted this paragraph, one which alters the whole atmosphere of the scene, it was he who guided my hand.

That was a good sign; it proved that he was truly alive. I would not say the same of Davis. Davis is a manufactured character. You can tell. I'm perfectly aware of it. There's just one passage that gives him a breath of life: "He [Castle] was glad that the face showed no indication of pain. He drew the pyjamas together across the hollow chest. A button was missing." But the poor chap was already dead. When all is said and done, Davis only came alive after his death' (*Carnet rouge*).*

When Graham, who was always precise about detail, reread this passage in my diary, he added in his own hand, 'The trouble with my eyes comes not from the concentration upon a character, but on a character's movements. It's not important for the narrative that I mention that he sits down or goes to the window, but it's important for me that I follow his every movement' (*Carnet rouge*). It was this lively eye, which tracked his characters like a camera, which made the transposition of his books to the screen that much easier, as Carol Reed and Peter Glenville, in particular, have observed.

Soizic: So the work tired him, but was he not pleased, all the same, after making the effort?

Yvonne: Not necessarily. It all depended on the actual results of these efforts. What is more, where he and his writing were concerned, Graham was far too exacting in his standards to allow even the slightest satisfaction to compensate for his exhaustion. It stemmed from his character. He was never pleased with himself, and he put it like this: 'For a writer, and similarly for a priest, there is no such thing as success. I always think I could do better; that I ought to do better' (*Carnet rouge*).

* This conversation took place at the end of September 1978 at Il Passetto restaurant in Rome when we were on our way to Capri. *The Human Factor* had just been published.

Soizic: Apart from Graham's deep-rooted dissatisfaction, wasn't there the dread of the blank page, not to mention the writer's block, that threatens one insidiously?

Yvonne: Mainly, he used to tell me about the feeling of agonising loneliness that he experienced when confronted with a blank page, as compared to working in a team, which was something he had experienced when working with the director and the cast on the production of his play *The Return of A. J. Raffles* (1975), for instance. That was truly a holiday for him.

Soizic: Did this anxiety contribute to his writer's block?

Yvonne: No, the writer's block is just one of those stumbling-blocks, a phenomenon which is unavoidable. Almost every writer experiences it. It's terrifying for them. Suddenly, there's this void, this black hole. And it can last for three or four days. Like going through a tunnel where they can't see the end.

Soizic: Was this a problem that Graham often had to confront?

Yvonne: Much too often, for it was terribly traumatic every time. For example, when he was writing *The Honorary Consul* he had a sudden block. He had already written two-thirds of the book and he really thought he would have to abandon it. He was driven to despair and he said, 'I can understand how Hemingway came to fire a bullet through his brain. It's the only way out' (*Carnet rouge*).

I watched him, sitting there, on the brink of despair, collapsed into an armchair. Then, all of a sudden, he stood up and uttered the magic words: 'Back to the wall, Greene.'

The following night, he had a dream, which enabled him to escape from his writer's block (see *A World of My Own*, p. 59). The idea of abandoning the novel was intolerable to him.

Soizic: What other aspects of his 'job' used he to talk about?

Yvonne: Possibly one of the most specific and fascinating aspects was the constant and haunting presence of some of the characters he had created and the relationship he had with them afterwards. This arose from the fact that he took them very seriously and he literally lived alongside Scobie, say, or Castle, or Harry Lime . . . 'During my life I have spent more time living with fictional characters than with real people,' he sometimes said.

One morning, he appeared in the doorway, looking extremely worried, and announced quite abruptly, 'It's terrible to think that from now on I'm going to have to live for three years with a certain Charlie Fortnum.' And then he went back to whatever he was doing, without saying another word.

He had just begun writing *The Honorary Consul* (published in 1973).

A few years later, he discovered that comment, which I had recorded in my diary, and he wrote in the margin, 'I am surprised at that reflection, but perhaps I was remembering how depressed I was when I had to endure the company of Querry in writing *A Burnt-Out Case*. In fact, I grew quite attached to Charlie Fortnum' (*Carnet rouge*).

This simple episode shows that his characters existed outside himself, as real and living independent people, and that he could continue to alter his opinion of them.

Soizic: But weren't these instances when his world spilt over into reality and into your life together rather rare, given his temperament? Didn't he lock himself away, in fact, with his 'creatures', in his very secret writer's world?

Yvonne: His reference to Charlie Fortnum was actually an exception. One thing is certain: he never normally talked about a book while he was working on it.

Soizic: Why was that, do you think?

Yvonne: Because he was much too aware of the dangers that any intrusion might have for his subconscious or on his source of inspiration; for the smooth-running but fragile mechanism that enabled him to bring his books to life. He would not countenance any interruption to his creative work that was not of his making and his alone.

Soizic: And yet your private diary shows evidence of many a conversation about his writings. One might even say that they are its principal preoccupation.

Yvonne: The selection I have made in the diary may perhaps distort the reality; we were actually very eclectic and spontaneous in our choice of conversations; many of them were to do with current affairs or with the copious amount of post he received. Nevertheless, his work as a writer must have been central to our discussions, for I had much to learn in this field, which was one that fascinated me, and so I asked numerous questions on the subject.

I still remember very clearly a discussion we had during my first visit to Capri in July 1967:* we were dining at his favourite restaurant, Chez Gemma. I was determined to make him talk about himself – not about the man, but about the writer – and I asked him the following question:

'If you were to label yourself in literary terms, how would you classify yourself?'
Graham: 'I'm neither a theorist, nor a philosopher. I'm a storyteller.'
'What exactly do you mean by that?'
Graham: 'A storyteller creates characters first of all, and

---

* Graham owned a villa at Anacapri (Capri), which was his favourite place in which to work. Later, we used to go there frequently.

he then proceeds to make them speak and tell an interesting story. Among my predecessors, I would mention Robert Louis Stevenson – *Treasure Island* – Conrad and, in his way, Henry James, whom I admire very much. Whenever I feel discouraged, I reread him and that gives me fresh impetus.'

In the margins of my *Carnet rouge*, in which I recorded this conversation, he added: 'Stevenson made the storyteller respectable in literature. I still admire his successors and have them on my shelves: Anthony Hope, Stanley Weyman, Conan Doyle and E. W. Hornung (creator of Raffles).'

I remember this discussion on general matters as an exception. I tended to be more curious about the technical details of writing: the little quirks and the superstitions that I suppose are inherent in any creative enterprise, the preconceived ideas that betray the creator's anxieties.

Soizic: Can you give some examples?

Yvonne: I could give you examples galore, for Graham was a very superstitious man, both in life and also therefore in his books. This aspect of him became apparent to me during a conversation about his early work. Apart from the first book to be published, *The Man Within* (1929), which achieved a certain critical success at least, the two that followed, *The Name of Action* (1930) and *Rumour at Nightfall* (1931), were failures, as you know. It was a bitter pill. After long meditation, he came to the conclusion that their failure was due to his lack of experience, certainly, but above all to the principal characters in these novels: Chant in the former, and Chase and Crane in the latter, all had names beginning with the letter C. He saw this as a sort of curse and decided to abandon the ill-starred letter.*

---

* As he eventually admitted to me, the ghost of Carter, his *bête noire* at Berkhamsted, still haunted his subconscious.

Many years later, after a passing temptation to use the initial, as we can see from *In Search of a Character* (1961), he used it again in *The Human Factor* (1978), where the name Castle imposed itself as an obvious one, giving the lie to all his misgivings.

Apart from the names of the characters, the title of a book and its epigraph were essential considerations in his eyes. In fact, by the time he had made up his mind on these two points, he already had some of the important lines of the new novel fixed in his head.

He always bitterly regretted that his American publisher altered the title of *The Power and the Glory* to *The Labyrinthine Ways*, which to his mind did not reflect the spirit of the book at all. That happened in 1941, and he was obliged to accede to his publisher's demands. In 1971 however, when Viking Press informed his literary agent, Monica McCall, that they wanted to change the title of *Travels with My Aunt* – which was apparently not commercial in the United States – to 'Aunt Augusta', Graham flew into a rage and sent off a telegram saying, 'Would rather change publisher than title. Graham Greene.' Without further ado, he kept his word: he left Viking Press, to the great dismay of Tom Ginzburg, the firm's managing director, and found a new home at Simon & Schuster.*

This kind of sudden reaction was also part of his personality. He could be impulsive and impatient, not allowing himself the time to think before acting, even if it meant regretting it afterwards.

Soizic: And did he regret the angry moods you've just described?

Yvonne: Above all, he felt a profound bitterness, for he maintained friendly relations with all his publishers and these meant

* He returned to Viking Press in 1984, with the publication of *Getting to Know the General*.

a great deal to him. His leaving Tom Ginzburg was extremely painful for him, but the episode is a proof of the symbiosis that existed in his mind between a novel and its title.

Soizic: You mentioned epigraphs, and I remember reading a remark of Graham's on the subject in your diary: 'The epigraph is meant to sum up what the book is all about.' Could you comment on that?

Yvonne: Well, I should like to describe the circumstances that gave rise to the remark. It was October 1978. *The Human Factor* had just been published in France; the epigraph to the novel is from Joseph Conrad: 'I only know that he who forms a tie is lost. The germ of corruption has entered into his soul.'

In *Le Figaro-Magazine* of 7 October 1978, Graham had come across an article by Anthony Burgess which said, among other things, 'Greene is in my view the best epigraphist in our business.'

Given that relationships between these fellow writers had already deteriorated somewhat, Graham was all the more surprised and flattered. He said to me, 'That remark pleases me very much and I accept it. I have always been very interested and attached great importance to a book's epigraph.'

But there's an element of magic and mystery about them, as the following two comments he wrote in my notebook reveal:

A mystery surrounds the epigraph by Tennyson I put at the beginning of *Getting to Know the General*. ['I go, but I return: I would I were/The pilot of the darkness and the dream.'] I was completely at a loss. I am not very fond of Tennyson and seldom read him. I opened a volume of his as a last resort and at random. The book opened at a long poem I had never read before and my eyes fell at once on the lines I used, which seemed perfectly to express my view of Omar Torrijos.

Or again:

> Another mystery: I find on the title page of my book of dreams a very opposite epigraph by Heraclitus of Ephesus, 500 BC. 'The waking have one world in common/ but the sleeping turn aside each/into a world of his own.' Where on earth did I pick that up?

Soizic: Did he talk readily about his books and did he make assessments of them?

Yvonne: Yes. No matter how reticent he was in talking about himself and about his private life, he was quite prepared to reply to questions about his work, as the numerous critics who interviewed him have observed. He was very severe on himself, but he was lucid, objective and impartial, ready to accept criticisms when he considered them justified, but upset and depressed if he reckoned they were stupid or, worse still, if they were clearly biased.

I once asked him, in a general way, the following question: of all your novels, which is the one you prefer? Graham replied, 'It's hard to answer that question, because in each of my novels there are things I like and others that I dislike; but if I had to make a choice, I think it would be *The Honorary Consul* (1973).' And he continued, 'The reason why I like the book is that it shows characters changing through their experiences – especially Plarr and Fortnum – a difficult thing for me to bring off' (*Carnet rouge*). This occurred in 1976, before the publication of *The Human Factor*, *Dr Fischer of Geneva* and *Monsignor Quixote*, and his last fictional work, *The Captain and the Enemy*.

A few years later, leafing through my notebook and realising there was a gap here, he hastily filled it: 'Many years after this was written, other books have been born. I now think [no date is given] I might choose *Monsignor Quixote* (1982).' He was then seventy-eight. The book, whose principal theme is doubt and its virtues, certainly corresponded with his state of mind at that time, when he used to describe himself as a 'Catholic agnostic'. It was also a period when he dreamt of a rapprochement between an updated – humanised – Communism and a Catholicism which was more open to the realities of life, and for which the burgeoning friendship between a communist mayor and a priest served as a symbol. He therefore found himself totally 'in phase' with his subject at last; and what a long road it had been since the publication of *A Burnt-Out Case* (1961) which, in his mind, was going to bring his career as a writer to an end.

10

Reality and Fiction

Soizic: In previous chapters we have touched on the autobiographical aspect of Graham Greene's work, something which has unquestionably given rise to fierce and often contradictory controversy. For some, 'Graham Greene's work can be read as a virtually undisguised autobiography';* others attribute an element of universality to it that enables everybody to identify with this or that character. Which interpretation accords with your own view?

Yvonne: The latter, definitely. My criteria for this are based on two factors: substance and technique.

As far as substance is concerned, it seems to me that the essential themes of his books – life and death, politics and religion, love and hatred – confer a universal character on his books, in which each one of us can feel involved.

As for technique, he denied that there was anything missionary or didactic about his work. 'I am not a preacher, still less a pedagogue,' he often used to say. Of course, his books often raise real questions of the kind that each of us is bound to ask ourselves sooner or later, but they don't impose any response and therefore leave the reader free to make his own choice. This feeling of self-identification is perfectly illustrated by the following note from one of his American correspondents. This is the gist of it:

* Victor de Pange, *Graham Greene* (Paris: Editions Universitaires, 1952), with a preface by François Mauriac.

Dear Mr Greene,

Thank you so very much for your many, many pages of marvellous writing: a rich source of ideas for contemplation, amusement and everything between. My special favourite is *Travels with My Aunt*. I've read it a good twenty times. It has guided me through several years of challenging changes, not unlike Henry Pulling's. It has been a blessing on my life. Thank you so much.

When he handed me the letter, which was dated 13 November 1990, Graham said, 'Keep it, and when you read it remember that it gave me a moment of great happiness.'

Soizic: Did he talk to you about the way he saw things?

Yvonne: Graham saw things from the inside. It was a subject which cropped up frequently in our conversations, and it became quite clear that, for him, the reality we experience must first sink into the unconscious – become 'obliterated' – in order to provide a compost which is unidentifiable with its creation, so that, to his way of thinking, the straightforward 'copy' of reality, or even the simple projection of his own personality, was no longer possible. He explained the process to me one day in these terms: 'I have the capacity to forget a secret which has just been confided in me the moment afterwards. I think I would have made a good priest. But this ability to forget is also a precious gift for the novelist; it's a weapon against sterility.' And he went on to clarify what he meant: 'I suppose what is forgotten sinks into the unconscious and is enriched there, so that it rises again with all the excitement of novelty' (*Carnet rouge*).

This is actually the very opposite of those theories according to which his work was nothing but a reflection of his life, theories he was determined to refute, as the letter addressed as a dedication to his friend Frere, in his novel *The Comedians* (1966), proves:

Many readers assume – I know it from experience – that an 'I' is always the author. So in my time I have been considered the murderer of a friend, the jealous lover of a civil-servant's life, and an obsessive player of roulette . . . 'I' is not the only imaginary character: none of the others, from such minor players as the British chargé d'affaires to the principals, has ever existed. A physical trait taken here, a habit of speech, an anecdote . . . are boiled up in the kitchen of the unconscious and emerge unrecognizable even to the cook in most cases.

That letter to a friend – a great friend – confirms my view that his books were, first and foremost, works of creation.

Soizic: But then what about the autobiographical element in fiction that you mentioned?

Yvonne: He gave the answer to your question himself in *A Sort of Life*, when he wrote, 'A writer's knowledge of himself, realistic and unromantic, is like a store of energy on which he must draw for a lifetime: one volt of it properly directed will bring a character alive . . .' From which one can conclude that the true essence of the characters in his fiction was his subconscious, and that everything was based on introspection, something he had begun to practise from the age of sixteen onwards.

Soizic: And yet in *Ways of Escape*, he told us:

> The main characters in a novel must necessarily have some kinship to the author, they come out of his body as a child comes from the womb, then the umbilical cord is cut, and they grow into independence. The more the author knows of his own character the more he can distance himself from his invented characters and the more room they have to grow in.

Isn't there a contradiction with what has previously been said?

Yvonne: The contradiction is only apparent when one looks at the way characters are developed, a process described explicitly in *In Search of a Character*, where we watch their slow evolution, the hesitations, the search for the right name, one which is perfectly suited to the role allotted to such and such a character in his mind. Then comes the moment when, once all this has been organised, 'the plane takes off' – an image he often used as a symbol for characters achieving their independence.

Soizic: Do you mean by that that they escape from their creator's control?

Yvonne: Not only do they escape from his control, but they impose their own will. The author actually becomes hostage to the characters he himself has created.

Soizic: What was it that helped you to understand those processes and speak so positively about them?

Yvonne: He explained them to me himself.

Soizic: In what circumstances?

Yvonne: Oh well, the unexpected turns that conversations take between two people are sometimes strange. For example, I still wonder what could have led to my questioning him on 16 February 1988, in his flat in Antibes, in the following way:
'You are undeniably a "man of instinct" far more than a "man of reason". What connection would you make, in this context, between the man and the writer?'

Graham: 'I believe that this is really the basis for all my work. The general term "writer" is used to refer to people who practise totally different functions. I would make three essential distinctions. There are historians, whose work is based on actual facts and events; there are the theoreticians, who provide an intellectual interpretation of those facts, and who then develop theories; and, finally, there are the writers of the imagination. I belong to this last group, and I am certain that "emotion" has an enormous amount to do with the creation of fictional characters. The only means of bringing them to life is to imagine how they would behave in a given situation. That's where the emotional element comes in: in order to describe the impact of events on a particular character, and his subsequent reactions, I need to experience a genuinely deep emotion myself in the same circumstances and confronted with a similar situation' (*Carnet rouge*).

Soizic: What a commitment, and it's limitless, what's more . . .

Yvonne: That's really what gives such depths to the notion of 'suffering' linked to writing, which we have previously discussed, and which he expressed in these terms: 'Fifty years of living with fictional characters, of dreaming their dreams, picking up their jealousies, meannesses, dishonest tricks of thoughts and betrayals doesn't make one easy to live with.'

He observed this same phenomenon of characters transferring their emotions and imposing them on their creator among other 'writers of the imagination'. On the subject of Flaubert, he wrote, 'You can see him becoming Madame Bovary, developing in himself her destructive passion' (*Ways of Escape*).

Soizic: Flaubert actually said, '*Madame Bovary, c'est moi.*' Did Graham, to your mind, go as far as Flaubert did in his intense and paradoxical efforts to become 'the other' while still being himself?

Yvonne: That's actually where the real paradox of literary creation lies; but to try to unravel the incredibly complicated process of writing is a bit like trying to elucidate the mysterious alchemy of life itself, for that's what we're talking about. The only answer I can give to your question is that, taken individually, I don't recognise the man I knew and loved in any of Graham's fictional characters. It is nevertheless undeniable that each one of his books reflected his state of mind at a given moment in his life.

Soizic: Conversely, have you ever felt there was a connection between any of his female characters and yourself? Between reality and fiction?

Yvonne: Just one character comes to mind with any certainty. It's a comment by Brown – the main character in *The Comedians* – about his mistress, Martha. This is what he says: 'I realized and appreciated her directness. She played no part. She answered exactly what I asked. She never claimed to like a thing that she disliked or to love something to which she was indifferent.'* This discreetly sketched portrait of a woman struck me as being so familiar that it was impossible for me not to identify with her, even if the setting had changed. Even today those words ring in my ears like an echo of the past.

Soizic: Did you tell him of your discovery?

Yvonne: Yes, of course. He made no comment. He just smiled. But that smile said a great deal . . .

There was one other occasion, in my view, when fiction caught up with reality and when I identified myself so totally with one of his characters that I finished reading the book deeply upset and in tears. It was to do with the passage at the very end of *The Human Factor* (1978), in which two characters who love one another, Castle and his wife Sarah, are separated

---

* Part One, Chapter 5, 2.

for ever, in their two very different worlds, and they only become aware of this the very moment that their telephone conversation is mercilessly cut off. When he realised from my reaction how upset I was, Graham came up to me and said, 'Don't worry, my darling, between us there will never be a dead line. We will go together in a plane crash.'

That was the day when I became fully aware that he was nineteen years older than me, and it was the first time that the spectre of our possible separation appeared to me in all its horror.

Soizic: But how could he, who was so happy with you in real life (in spite of the 'spectre', which no doubt hovered in the background for him, too), conceive of such a tragedy, even in a novel?

Yvonne: It's a very good example of the way he could separate fiction from reality. On his own admission, he never succeeded in constructing a novel with living characters in it.

Soizic: Why was that, do you think?

Yvonne: He used to say that it was because no one can know anyone else completely; every human being has his or her own 'secret garden' which is by definition unfathomable. To try to construct a character in a novel based on an actual person inevitably results in mutilation, and the character becomes incomplete, bland and not very credible. As far as he was concerned, paradoxical though it may seem, the only way of creating living characters in their own right was to assemble them piecemeal, and to invest them, in his imagination, with the natural instincts – both good and bad – that lie hidden within each one of us.

Soizic: Can you affirm that he never wrote a book about real people, even if he was tempted to do so? Hadn't he considered writing a book about my father, for example, even assembling documents with this in mind?

Yvonne: I won't affirm it, for the good reason that he did, in fact, write a book about real people. The main character in that book, which he called *Getting to Know the General*, was to have been Omar Torrijos – the strongman of Panama in the years 1970–80 – whose charismatic personality had attracted Graham ever since their first meeting in 1974. But an intruder called Chuchu intervened, and his very colourful personality meant that the General was relegated to second place.*

'That book was a mistake,' Graham used to say irritably. 'Never, never again.'

Soizic: Taking your argument a stage further, would you say that everything in his novels is the pure product of his imagination?

Yvonne: No, certainly not. We have been talking solely about the characters in his fiction. They are merely the actors in this tragi-comedy called life; real life – at least, to his way of thinking.

Soizic: Don't you think it's because his vision of the world is actually so idiosyncratic that some have dubbed it 'Greeneland'?

Yvonne: To those people he replied, 'Those who speak of "Greeneland" go about with their eyes shut.' In fact, he couldn't bear people questioning the veracity of his comments about events or facts that he had witnessed first-hand, for even though he allowed free rein to his imagination in a fictional

* Chuchu, whose real name was José Jesús Martínez, was Torrijos's bodyguard and accompanied Graham Greene on his travels in Panama.

context, he was, on the other hand, extremely scrupulous about precise details in his descriptions of backgrounds, and particularly so when he was reporting on them, as was the case with *The Quiet American* (1955), which was about the French war in Vietnam, and, of course, *The Comedians* (1966), set in Haiti during the rule of Dr Duvalier.

Soizic: We cannot end this chapter without mentioning Graham's skills as a 'storyteller', a talent acknowledged by all, even his detractors. Did you ever raise the subject with him?

Yvonne: He was far too modest to speak about it; but he accepted that type of compliment, which he thought was justified.

He revealed his concept of the art of storytelling to me shortly before his death and entirely fortuitously. He came up to me one day carrying a book entitled *The Letters of Ezra Pound*.* It was Graham's bedside book until the end of his life. The following passage is one he read to me and it's an extract from a letter from Pound to a friend, Harriet Monroe, dated January 1915: 'Language is made out of concrete things. General expressions in non-concrete terms are a laziness, they are talk, not art, not creation. They are the reaction of things on the writer, not a creative act *by* the writer.'

'You see,' he told me, 'I should have liked to have written that, for it expresses my opinion on the art of storytelling exactly.'

* *The Letters of Ezra Pound, 1907–41*, edited by D. D. Paige (London: Faber and Faber, 1950).

I I

The Helper in the Shadows

Soizic: Among the many books by Graham you possess, two are dedicated to you. *Travels with My Aunt*, dedicated to H. H. K., which we have already discussed, and his last work of fiction, published in 1988, *The Captain and the Enemy*, in which he wrote: 'For Y with all the memories we share of nearly thirty years.' Apart from those two particularly important dedications, all his other books on your shelves are variously inscribed, and they all have this in common: they display his gratitude for the help you gave him. On the flyleaf of the French edition of *May We Borrow Your Husband?* (1967), for example: 'For Yvonne, who worked so hard getting the translation right and whose name should be on the front page, with love from Graham'; or, in the French version of *Ways of Escape* (1983): 'For Yvonne, who helped so much with the translation, with love from Graham.' I've noticed seven inscriptions of this type, even though you probably had a hand in other books as well. Did you have a practical role to play? If we are to believe Graham's inscriptions, you put in a lot of work.

Yvonne: It's true, I worked very hard. Since I was with him from midday onwards (he wrote until then), I used to get down to work at night. Especially on the translations. They always had to be done quickly. Of course, Graham was sent the translated text. He knew enough French to pick up certain expressions which displeased him. Occasionally, he came across enormous errors, which he noted down. Above all, he sometimes felt that there was a lack of pace, and he often found that the French translation was, to his way of thinking, 'pedestrian'. At times like that, we would discuss it together, and I had to try to moderate the style. He used to say that a translation should be 'literary', not 'literal'. I could influence what was written in so far as I knew Graham so well, particularly the way he expressed himself. So it was not something I could have done for anyone else. The French edition of *Getting to Know the General*, for example, is full of anecdotes he had already told me, so I was familiar with the context. And when I got stuck, I, in turn, would appeal to 'the master' for help! He had extraordinary patience – the patience of an angel – over things like that. He was always cooperative, and he never complained when I sought his help in solving a difficulty, however burdensome, because for all their deceptive simplicity – the straightforward words, and his lightness of style – Graham's books are actually very hard to translate, at least into French. 'They're stuffed full of traps,' Georges Belmont once told me.* As for Marcelle Sibon, she decided to call it a day after translating *May We Borrow Your Husband?*, in which the strange, contemporary language of the title story – the sort used in homosexual milieux – was totally alien to her.† That's why, at the request of Marie Biche, who was Graham's French literary agent at the time, I was originally persuaded to work on the text of a translation.

I enjoyed doing it, and I found it hard to drag myself away, to such a point that it almost became an obsession.

---

* Georges Belmont was the translator of *Travels with My Aunt* (1970), *The Honorary Consul* (1973) and *The Human Factor* (1978), in collaboration with Hortense Chabrier. All were published by Robert Laffont, Paris.
† Marcelle Sibon translated all Graham Greene's books from *Brighton Rock* in 1947 up to *The Comedians* in 1966, also published by Robert Laffont.

Soizic: Would you say that that was the principal practical role you played during the last twenty-five years and more of Graham's life? Did you involve yourself in any editing, in the translation of titles, or even the choosing of titles?

Yvonne: Yes, I would say it kept me very busy. Where titles were concerned, I would put ideas for translations to him. The final choice was his, obviously. But in this way I came up with *À la rencontre du Général* (*Getting to Know the General*), *Les Chemins de l'évasion* (*Ways of Escape*), and finally *Mon univers secret* (*A World of My Own*).

Soizic: The last of those books is one you edited, isn't it?

Yvonne: Yes. Before he died, Graham asked me to prepare the book for publication. It was a job he wasn't able to complete, and which I was able to do with the invaluable help of his niece Louise Dennys, who's a publisher in Toronto.*
   I also looked after all his correspondence in French.
   All in all, I would say that my practical role tended to be that of a helper in the shadows.

Soizic: Did you feel equally involved in his creative work?

Yvonne: No, certainly not. I never had access to it. I was never an inspiration or any sort of 'poetic muse' for him – not that he believed in such myths, in any case. Where his creative work was concerned, he depended solely upon himself, and he used to isolate himself completely from the outside world so as to inhabit 'a world of his own'.
   Conversely, my role, as I saw it, was precisely that of an assistant; someone who could offer a friendly hand to help him

---

* Louise Dennys, executive publisher, Alfred A. Knopf, and executive vice-president of Random House, Canada. She was the editor of *Ways of Escape* and *Monsignor Quixote*.

emerge from his isolation and rediscover the comfort and warmth he needed so badly. I even used to see myself sometimes as a St Bernard, so lost did he seem when he surfaced from his hours of labour. What's more, at times like that he himself used to say that I was his 'reward', a sentiment he expressed in any number of letters, when he said, 'You can't imagine how much help and comfort you give me.'

Soizic: Did this 'help' and 'comfort' have any repercussions on the man and his life, in your opinion?

Yvonne: There you're asking me to be both judge and jury in an extremely subjective and delicate area, in which the only reference points I have are what has been observed and expressed by the people he knew, his relations and friends.

Soizic: But what exactly is your own personal view?

Yvonne: I believe I brought him a certain stability which he hadn't known before. The length of our relationship is proof of that, and he himself was aware of it when he said to me, 'I have always been cyclothymic. In the past, I used to go through bouts of deep depression, followed by a period of great euphoria. It appears that I have now reached a plateau' (*Carnet rouge*). This notion of a 'plateau' became apparent during the seventies. Many of his oldest friends noticed the change and they shared their observations with me.

Furthermore, his letters, I remember vividly, bear traces of his own astonishment when he uses terms such as the French word '*sage*' – it's one that reappears frequently over the long years, but particularly at the beginning: 'I was completely *sage*'; '*Je suis complètement sage*. I have no curiosity. No desire for anyone but you'; 'I feel rather spiritless. All the love in the world from your *sage* and lonesome lover.'

Soizic: Wasn't that to reassure you about the sort of life that an adventurer like him might lead when he was far away from you on his travels?

Yvonne: No, not exactly. It was to put me off the scent. It was actually he who most needed to be reassured. '*Je suis complètement sage*', I am convinced, corresponded to the reality, but it was also evidence of a certain anxiety in his mind, of a need to be reassured about my conduct while he was away. He was the one who was tormented and anxious by temperament. To begin with, his worries revealed themselves very discreetly, as, for example, when he wrote to me from Bombay in that same year: 'I hope that you didn't fall in love with a handsome stranger because your ugly lover is very much in love with you'. Then, with reference to the 'adventurer' side of him, he wrote to me from Kingston, in Jamaica: 'My darling, I am living a restless life geographically, but I am *completely sage*. You really have destroyed my interest in adventures.' And in a another letter, during the same trip, though by then en route for Haiti and *The Comedians*, he added, dismissing the 'geographical' aspect for a moment: 'I get in awful moods of melancholy and doom . . . I'm tired of travelling . . . It's too long to wait' (20 July 1963).

Soizic: The lover who is '*sage*', therefore, but impatient, and who champs at the bit . . . The absence of '*sagesse*' – the obsession – dwelling, of course, 'at home', you being his harbour . . . How very often, in fact, in these loving letters, physical passion reveals itself in startling fashion! 'I've got a *cafard terrible* and feel tired and flat. With you I didn't feel tired and flat'.

Would you say, therefore, that your mutual sensuality, which is something one senses very strongly, was the essential element in your relationship?

Yvonne: Yes, certainly, particularly at the beginning. We had an overwhelming need for one another. It will come as no surprise to anyone that Graham was a sensual man. He himself admitted as much and wrote about it in his autobiography. He was sensual, certainly, but he wasn't a hedonist. He enjoyed the pleasures of the flesh, yet he was not a sybarite. As for me, I did, I think, have a talent for happiness . . .

Soizic: 'A talent for happiness.' Can you explain? Haven't you just revealed the key to the success of your life as a couple?

Yvonne: I believe I brought to his life something which is a predisposition, or rather a flair – call it a gift from the gods – by which I mean an intense *joie de vivre*. In this respect I was the very opposite of him. The antidote to his torments. He rather envied this ability I had and he aspired to the same serenity. I enshrined the happiness for which he yearned.

Soizic: Did this happiness rub off on him and, if so, how?

Yvonne: I believe I provided him with moments of peace, passing ones, at least, through that total and mutual gift of oneself which is called, quite appropriately, '*la petite mort*'.* In that way – it was a long-term process – I eventually managed to make him equate the word 'love' with 'joy' and 'happiness', and no longer with 'torments' and 'suffering'. For I understood his anxieties, I 'received' them. But my desire to help him was so strong that I resisted the temptation to sink into his gloom. So I slightly alleviated the world-weariness that he carried like a weight deep within him. Because he did not like himself, he had a desperate, unfathomable need to feel loved.

Soizic: And he was loved . . . How, exactly?

---

* Or, less romantically, in English: the moment of sexual fusion [Tr.].

Yvonne: As the years went by, I gave him back his self-confidence by giving him proof that I loved him. I made sure he trusted me by demonstrating that I was faithful to him. The finest token of my 'success' in this connection is something he once said in a letter I remember by heart, of course, and which I keep in me: 'I *know* how much I love you. I have never felt so close or so certain with any other woman. I'm sure of you and sure of myself as I've never been.' It was in December 1972.

Soizic: We're a long way here from the Graham of the Thomas the Doubter days . . . In your view, what were some of the other repercussions of this hitherto undisclosed serenity on his behaviour?

Yvonne: The most radical and spectacular change in him was unquestionably in the realm of jealousy: that type of obsessive, irrational jealousy from which he had suffered so much in the past and which is revealed so clearly as an aberration in *The End of the Affair*. That novel, universally recognised as being the most overtly theological of his books, presents us with a lover, Bendrix, who is so jealous of his mistress, Sarah, that he invents pretexts for justifying his behaviour and poisoning her life. It is only when a private diary is found after Sarah's death that he is brought back to reality and made to realise that his rival was none other than God himself, an abstract being, in other words.

Soizic: Didn't he to some extent rid himself of that 'suffering' precisely by writing the book?

Yvonne: It was one of the novels we spoke about most often. He almost regretted having written it, so distressing were the interpretations put on it by both critics and the public. It's true that he did provide a few sticks to beat himself with: the fact that Bendrix was also a writer, etc., etc. To me, that only proves that when he wrote the novel he was partially cured. But, as one notices from his letters written up to the sixties, his dread of betrayal had existed for a long time and no one should believe that the expressions 'I was *sage*, completely *sage*' or 'I hope you are *sage*, too', however cheerful they sound, were as anodyne as they may seem. He realised that what I shall call 'the game of bidding high', which he had allowed himself to play in the past, could lead only to disaster. And finally, very gradually, he came to the following conclusion: 'I now realise that within a couple jealousy is actually nothing but the projection of one's own follies on the other. We attribute to the other person those things that we feel guilty about in ourselves. In some way it's a "safety valve"' (*Carnet rouge*). He doesn't mention jealousy again in his later books.

Soizic: Did this new stability have any effect on his work, do you think?

Yvonne: Yes, certainly. You only have to look at *Travels with My Aunt* to realise what they were. This totally jubilant novel, which deals with the serious subject of death, is a reflection of the period of intense euphoria he went through at the time. It is also proof of the fact that Graham, who had always convinced himself that he could be creative only when he was troubled or suffering, could also create when he was happy. But that was a unique case among his books, because it corresponded to a period of transition between excessive worry and the gradual tranquillity that followed.

Soizic: Can you see any other consequences of this evolution on Graham's work as a writer?

Yvonne: A new tendency seems to have emerged in those years, marking a shift in his main interests towards politics and away from religion.

Soizic: How do you explain that?

Yvonne: Obviously I can't be certain, but, from what he told me, religion belonged to a past he wanted to forget, whereas politics had to do with the present. Furthermore, we had far more mutual interests on a political level. Graham was aware of that, for he once told me, in the early seventies, 'My main areas of interest in life have always been religion and politics. In the old days, religion was more dominant. Nowadays, I have clearly opted for politics.' *The Comedians*, *The Honorary Consul* and *The Human Factor* are illustrations of this new tendency, although *Monsignor Quixote* remains an exception.

Soizic: Would you say that over the years, simply through love or imitation, you 'rubbed off' on one another? Your daughter Martine, talking about Graham, said that 'he couldn't survive without you'.

Yvonne: You're talking about a dependence that was inevitable. I couldn't have survived without him, either. If that is the price one pays for happiness, it was one we were glad to accept.

Soizic: We have spoken about the effect you had on Graham. What changes did he bring about in you? Were you aware of any?

Yvonne: Rather than speak of changes, I would call it a veritable transformation. At the time I first met him, I had just spent fourteen years in Africa, almost cut off from the realities of life and enclosed in a world of selfishness and indifference. He opened my eyes to the outside world. He taught me everything about the things that make up life. He led me into a world of rich intimacy, both moral and spiritual. Above all, he made me more aware of the sufferings of others. I still remember a remark he made: 'The only people to have souls are those who are capable of suffering for others, even if it's only once in their lives.' He gave me a soul.

Soizic: Would you say that the experience had been a total success, then?

Yvonne: Yes, though with one reservation.

Soizic: What is that?

Yvonne: I was never able to reconcile him to himself. But that would have been an impossible mission.

12

Speaking Up for the Victims

The positions Graham Greene adopted in defence of human rights are well known and explicitly illustrated in numerous letters to the press, articles, reviews and lectures he gave, as well as in several books (for instance, *Yours etc.*, *Commitments*). They pervade his work with what one critic has called 'that tenacious, desperate compassion for the eternal human victim'.*

One may wonder, indeed, in some awe, at Greene's very special gift of sensitivity, added to an indomitable capacity and determination to take action, beyond the hollow talk or sympathies displayed in congresses and forums. 'Talk', he said, 'is so often an escape from action – instead of a prelude to action.' But Greene's 'simple' awareness of the existence, around the world or on his doorstep, of human misfortune lies at the core of his interest in human rights. Their defence was not yet quixotic in the days of perestroika, Prague's 'Velvet Revolution' or liberation theology . . . Yet that special fibre was already perceptible in Greene's earliest piece of reporting, in Dublin in 1923, just as it is, for instance, in his still very inspiring novel *The Quiet American*, which, as the American writer Gloria Emerson once told us, revealed Graham's 'absolute determination to help the Vietnamese'. These are examples of what 'matured into the political consciousness that gave moral urgency to his

* Vernon Young, 'The political Graham Greene speaks his mind', *Philadelphia Inquirer*, 29 May 1983.

fiction'.* His last novel, *The Captain and the Enemy*, mixes both the 'human factor' and the political one. Greene was consistent in his attitude, even at personal risk sometimes, beyond fiction: his pamphlet *J'Accuse* not only *de facto* denounced a climate of corruption on the Riviera, but was also written, as he put it, with the aim of helping friends 'out of a drama' in which 'they were unwittingly involved'. Not only was the pamphlet suppressed for being an intrusion into private life under French law, but he and his friends were 'threatened' for years 'by the criminal world of Nice'.†

For Graham, compassion was never very far away: 'Yes,' he explained again in 1985, 'the victims change – geographically and politically. At one moment one's sympathy is directed towards the inhabitants of the *gulag*s, on another to the victims of American policy in Central America, and on another, let us say, to the victims of Amin in Africa . . . But I don't think necessarily of the political victims – the writer always has to have sympathy with the victims of domestic trouble, of things touching human life in his immediate environment. It's only if one happens, as I have done, to travel a great deal and to get interested in the political aspects of a number of countries that such aspects come out. My first book about Latin America was *The Power and the Glory*, where the victims were the Catholics, and they awoke an imaginative sympathy which came out in a novel . . . But, as I say, I think Human Rights are also on the purely human, local level: a beggar on the streets, a woman who has been betrayed in some way, a man who has been betrayed . . .'‡

Soizic: How do you explain Graham's gift for sympathy, Yvonne? What, in your opinion, are its most impressive aspects?

* Judith Adamson *Reflections* (London: Reinhardt & Booker, 1990).
† The pamphlet *J'Accuse* was published by Bodley Head in 1982.
‡ *Le Monde diplomatique*, June 1985.

Yvonne: Having been marked by the humiliations he endured when he was very young, throughout his life Graham always played an active role, for he was very much aware of anything that violated human dignity. This was acknowledged unanimously.

It wasn't just by chance that he was so frequently invited to take part in debates on peace and the defence of human rights. I'm thinking of the Jerusalem Peace Prize, which he received in April 1981; of the Moscow conference he attended in February 1987; of the conference to commemorate the signing of the Helsinki Agreement in 1985, which enabled him to re-establish his personal commitment in this area.

Two examples come to mind which illustrate these remarks particularly well, especially since they are to do with his involving himself in a *collective* position, something unusual as far as he was concerned, for he generally took up an individual position.

In 1968 the invasion of Czechoslovakia by the Warsaw Pact troops drove him to add his name to the signatories of Charter 77. And in 1970 he took the step of resigning from the American Academy of Arts and Letters in order to protest against what he called 'the undeclared war' in Vietnam. At the same time, he became a member of the 272 Committee,* thereby confirming his disapproval.

Soizic: Why those particular examples?

Yvonne: Because they caused the greatest stir, but above all, in my view, because they show that Graham was capable of disregarding his own political beliefs the moment it became a question of fighting injustice.

In the first case, Graham, being, as we know, a man of the left, tended to sympathise naturally with the USSR. But the

---

* Members signed a petition against American intervention in Vietnam. Greene wrote and initiated the petition. According to Yvonne, 'The tract ended up in a dustbin after Graham's death.'

defence of those who had been attacked – namely, the citizens of Czechoslovakia – took priority over all other considerations. He therefore put his instinctive commitments to one side, without fear of going back on his decision. Václav Havel, incidentally, never forgot his gesture. I remember that one of Graham's greatest regrets at the end of his life (apart from his wish to go back to Cuba) was not to be able physically to go and meet him in Prague, where Havel had invited him. But they stayed in contact and remained friends until Graham's death.

As to American intervention in Vietnam and Graham's resignation, it was very different. Ever since the end of the French war in Indochina, Graham had in many different ways continued to condemn what he considered a disastrous trap. And at that moment, in 1970, he put his reputation at risk. For not only did he resign but he tried to persuade everyone he knew – writers, painters, sculptors – in the world of art and literature to do likewise. Very few of them responded to his pleas. I am thinking particularly of the reaction of François Mauriac, whose letter Graham showed me; Mauriac was prepared to commit himself to the principle, but first of all he wanted to know the names of the other people who were likely to resign . . .

Soizic: What triggered those stands?

Yvonne: Anger. An almost instinctive and instantaneous feeling of revolt that came over him. A sort of allergy, I would say. He admitted as much: 'It's the anger induced by what I saw in Vietnam, in Haiti, in Mexico, that made me write *The Quiet American*, *The Comedians* and *The Lawless Roads*. It's the people I spoke to, the on-the-spot witnesses, not the abstract principles or reported facts, that prompted this need to write which then became a necessity.'*

* *Le Monde diplomatique*, June 1985.

Speaking up for the victims took precedence over everything else. Graham then escaped from the constraints of his own political viewpoint – an attitude he expressed in the following terms: 'The writer should always be ready to change sides at the drop of a hat. He speaks up for the victims, and the victims change.'*

Soizic: Did you actually see him getting angry about a particular situation? Or was the anger white, cold and contained?

Yvonne: When an article he had read in a newspaper or a magazine shocked him, he used to react immediately and communicate his unreserved disapproval in a letter dictated to his secretary. In such cases, yes, taking immediate action was a sort of antidote to anger.

As you can imagine, such behaviour earned him a fair amount of hostility, but he didn't care, and nothing could stop him expressing himself, whatever the consequences might be.

Soizic: Did he always react so hastily?

Yvonne: No, certainly not. It all depended on the nature and the scale of the problem, naturally.

Soizic: What are you thinking of, more specifically?

Yvonne: I'm thinking of what I would call the bigger involvements: Vietnam, which we've already mentioned; Haiti; those in Central America: Panama and Nicaragua; South Africa. All countries he visited in order to study the situation for himself. He prepared his trips minutely and he always fixed up somewhere to stay beforehand, a 'point of contact', as he used to call it. It was Trevor Wilson in Vietnam, Bernard Diederich in Haiti;

* Shakespeare Prize acceptance speech, 'The Virtue of Disloyalty', Hamburg, 1969.

on his first journey to Panama in 1974, it was Chuchu who took charge; in South Africa, Étienne Leroux. They were all great friends, who prepared a precise sketch of the situation for him in advance and who accompanied him when he travelled around the country.

Soizic: Of all the struggles he was involved in, which do you think was the one that absorbed him the most?

Yvonne: Emotionally, it was undoubtedly Haiti. His relationship with the Haitians was a real love affair, one which began in 1954 and lasted until his death in 1991. It was actually news from Haiti that provided him with one of his last moments of joy: the democratic election of Father Jean-Bertrand Aristide, which put an end to almost thirty years – from 1957 to 1986 – of a bloody dictatorship imposed by the Duvalier dynasty, father and son.*

Graham's intense happiness was, however, mingled with sincere regret at not being able to participate in Aristide's investiture ceremony, to which he had been invited. From his hospital bed he asked me to send the new president the following telegram: 'Sorry not to be able to take up your invitation. Reasons of health. Your election is a great joy to me and an immense comfort. My sincere good wishes to you and to the people of Haiti. G. G.'

Soizic: Why such an intense and enduring attachment to an island which is virtually unknown in Europe?

---

* See Greene's introduction to the book by Bernard Diederich and Al Burt, *Papa Doc* (London: Bodley Head, 1970): 'No one alive (and the dead cannot speak from their unknown graves except to Papa Doc) is better qualified than Bernard Diederich to tell the terrifying story of Haiti under the rule of Dr François Duvalier . . . He had personal experience not only of the early Duvalier days but of what seems now by contrast to have been the golden period of [Paul] Magloire's rule; he is married to a Haitian and after his arrest and expulsion by Papa Doc, he followed the fortunes of his adopted country from across the border in Santo Domingo.'

Yvonne: Precisely because that ignorance and the world's indifference to such poverty were for him an additional incentive to take action, to denounce atrocities which should have concerned the conscience of the world.

When *The Comedians* was published, the Haitians expressed their gratitude in their own way by declaring, 'Graham Greene lightened the darkness of Haiti', or again, more humorously, more pathetically, 'After this, Haiti won't be mistaken for Tahiti any more.'

Soizic: Could it be said that it was the human factor that forged the commitment?

Yvonne: Not necessarily, no. Although it is true that the human factor – his instinctive sympathy – played an important part in the case we've just mentioned, he could also display the same fervour, the same determination to break the deadlock and come to the aid of a 'stranger' whose life or dignity were threatened, and I can attest to the fact that from his modest flat in Antibes he was in touch with all events in which his intervention was needed.

Soizic: Can you give some examples?

Yvonne: I'm thinking in particular of two kidnappings that occurred in El Salvador in 1980. The first was drawn to his attention during a telephone call from Gabriel García Márquez – incidentally, he did not recognise his voice immediately. The victims were delegates of the Bank of England, captured by Salvadorean guerrillas. The first step was to get in touch with the directors of the bank in order to obtain vital information about their two agents: their identities, the purpose of their mission to El Salvador and, if possible, the place where they were captured.

It was the beginning of long negotiations about the

conditions imposed by the guerrillas for the freeing of their hostages (the size of the ransom etc.), and endless conversations on the telephone, using Chuchu as the coordinator and inter-preter in the discussions. Once agreement was at last reached, the two businessmen were released unharmed, and together, with a few bottles of whisky, we celebrated the happy outcome of a tragic episode.

Soizic: Wasn't there a danger that during the negotiations you would have learnt everything about them?

Yvonne: My whole life with Graham was one long secret. I learnt to keep my mouth shut.

A few weeks later, anyway, there was a new alert, this time from Omar Torrijos, who sent to Antibes a young Panamanian who was ordered to deliver a secret envelope personally to Graham. In this particular case, it was to do with a South African ambassador who had also been taken captive by the Salvadorean rebels. Since resistance to oppression in that country had become more widespread and better organised, several groups of guer-rilla fighters now existed, and Graham, through the intermediary of Chuchu, had met some of their leaders in Nicaragua (he spoke to me mostly about a certain Gaetano, who had been captured and tortured by henchmen of José Duarte, who had recently been made president of El Salvador).

The problem was identifying which of the groups was responsible for the kidnapping.

Here again, Chuchu, Torrijos's right-hand man, was asked to make some inquiries on the spot and to establish some contacts. It took a great deal of time and skill to negotiate the conditions for freeing the ambassador, but they managed it, with Graham playing the role of the discreet but effective mediator.

Soizic: Don't you think that in that bottomless swamp, where the life of a human being was of little importance, they made use of Graham and his fame as a writer, for the sake of propaganda?

Yvonne: Of course. But for him the life of a human being was very important. Whatever the person's background or the colour of his or her skin. Human rights was for him a matter of principle from which nothing or no one could divert him, and if there was one area in which his celebrity assisted him, it was this.

The fact that some people made use of him for propaganda purposes was of little consequence. He was aware of this, and he used to retort, 'I couldn't care less if people make use of me to defend a cause in which I believe.' So true is this that when he visited Cuba for the last time in 1983, and Fidel Castro said to him, 'Well, Graham, what message have you brought me?' he replied, 'I have no message. I am the message.'

Soizic: Did all the struggles he became involved in have any effect or repercussions in your private life?

Yvonne: Yes, certainly, and for different reasons. As regards the case we've just mentioned, he kept me closely informed about what was happening and we shared all the emotions those human tragedies aroused. As to the repercussions, for a long time I felt a frustration which had to do with our being forced to abandon plans that had meant a lot to me.

Soizic: Can you be more precise?

Yvonne: He had always spoken to me very enthusiastically about the Soviet Union, which, ever since his adolescence, had exercised a sort of fascination for him. As soon as his financial situation allowed him to do so, he visited the country on several occasions and, through the Writers' Union in Moscow, formed friendships, especially among the intelligentsia. Ever since the beginning of our relationship, he had promised that one day he would allow me to discover a world which was totally alien to me.

I never imagined at the time that I would have to wait more than twenty years to realise what had become an unattainable dream.

Soizic: Why those long years of waiting?

Yvonne: The reason initially had to do with some unfortunate events which were to lead to a final break in Graham's relationships with his Soviet friends. In 1964, when he heard about the case of Yuri Daniel and Andreï Sinyavsky, two dissident writers who were sentenced respectively to five and seven years of forced labour for having published some of their books in the West, Graham asked that his author's royalties (which were blocked behind the Iron Curtain) be paid to their wives.

A firm and conclusive refusal of his request from the secretary-general of the Writers' Union came as such a shock that Graham replied immediately by prohibiting all future publication and translation of his books in the USSR.

The situation was at an impasse and relationships seemed to have been destroyed for good. But in the early eighties important changes were already noticeable in that country. In 1981, he received a new invitation from the Soviets. Spurred by curiosity, he was very tempted to accept. He was about to give in, but it so happened that in April 1981 he was to be awarded the Jerusalem Peace Prize, so we were invited to Israel. Graham was given a triumphant welcome by the authorities, and was received extremely warmly by the public.* Our visit was coming to an end, and on the eve of our departure, while we were in

* In the 1930s, Graham had not been spared by the wave of anti-Semitism prevalent in England at the time. This is apparent notably in *Brighton Rock*, albeit in a minor way.

the office of the mayor of Jerusalem, Teddy Kollek, the latter told Graham that the wife of the dissident Anatoly Shcharansky wanted to meet him. He agreed, and she was asked to come to the mayor's office. With great dignity, she told us the sad story of her life. Three years previously, in July 1978, she had been brutally separated from her husband the day after they were married. Anatoly had been put in prison, while she had been authorised to return to Israel, the country of her birth. Ever since then, she had fought to defend her husband's cause and to hasten his liberation. Graham, moved to tears, listened to her attentively and told her, 'There is, alas, little I can do for you, because this is the Soviet Union's internal affair. The only moral support I can give you is to cancel a trip I had planned to make shortly to that country and to give as the reason for my refusal our meeting here in Jerusalem and what you have just told me.'

As soon as we got back to France, he carried out his promise. It brought no results, alas: Shcharansky was not set free until February 1986. The incident in Jerusalem further postponed our trip to the USSR, because Graham stuck to his principles.

The years went by . . . The great changes expected in the USSR materialised with the advent of Mikhail Gorbachev in 1985. Perestroika came about, and glasnost began to pierce the wall of silence. Eventually Graham wanted to see for himself this 'socialism with a human face', which he had so long yearned for.

In the early summer of 1986 an official letter arrived signed by the new secretary-general of the Writers' Union inviting him to visit the country. He accepted, and asked me to accompany him.

On 5 September 1986 the dream in which I had stopped believing was realised at last, and I must admit that the reality far surpassed all my expectations. Graham radiated happiness: all his friends came to welcome him as he stepped down from the plane. A welcoming ceremony had been arranged in a private room at Sheremetyevo airport, with caviar and vodka, as they do in Moscow. The party had begun, and it continued throughout our stay in the USSR.

As to his royalties – the original reason for the conflict, blocked for twenty-two years in the vaults of a Moscow bank – Graham donated them all to the children who were victims of the recent catastrophe at Chernobyl, in April 1986.

Soizic: Was no shadow cast over this happiness, after so many vicissitudes and so many potential problems?

Yvonne: The quarrels of the past actually appeared to have been forgotten, and in all the euphoria of getting back on friendly terms Graham virtually agreed to take part in a round-table peace conference the Soviets planned for the following year. Then the umpteenth setback occurred: in *The Times* of 15 December 1986, Graham came across an article telling the particularly distressing story of Aleksander Ogorodnikov. According to *The Times*, this Orthodox dissident had managed to have a letter delivered to his mother in which he mentioned that during his seven years of detention he had gone on hunger strike for 659 days in order to have his Bible, and later his baptismal cross, returned to him. He had also spent ninety-one days in solitary confinement.

Graham was so indignant that in the heat of the moment he wrote the following letter to Henrick Borovick,* dated 17 December 1986:

> I very much regret that, after reading the enclosed article in *The Times* of 15 December, I feel it better to retire from your Round Table. Even as a bad Christian, I would feel it necessary to protest against the treatment of Aleksander Ogorodnikov.
>
> But my admiration and respect for Mr Gorbachev,

* Secretary-general of the Writers' Union at the time.

whom I am convinced knows nothing about this case, makes me very unwilling to protest publicly; nor do I wish to give pain to my many friends in the USSR.*

We did not have to wait long for a response. Borovick promised to give his full attention to Ogorodnikov's case and to contact the relevant authorities. A few days later, Graham obtained an assurance that the dissident had been freed. After that, there was nothing to prevent him taking part in the conference arranged by the Soviets in Moscow, which he visited in February 1987.

Soizic: As far as human rights were concerned, was the fact that he was particularly sensitive to the USSR due to his having been considered by many a 'fellow-traveller'?

Yvonne: Yes, I would say that he felt more directly involved in acts of violence perpetrated by his friends, and therefore more inclined to condemn their mistakes. Furthermore, in a letter to *The Times* dated 4 September 1967, he expressed his views clearly on this matter: 'But the greater the affection one feels for any country, the more one is driven to protest against any failure of justice there.'

But that's what Graham Greene was like: a man of action aware of the risks he was running and prepared to accept responsibility for them.

Soizic: Would you say he took responsibility for the risks that led him to write *J'Accuse*, or that he got caught in a sort of trap which could have been disastrous for him?

Yvonne: About *J'Accuse*, I just want to say that his commitment was not a political one. He simply could not remain mute in the

---

* Graham asked me to type the letter for him. I kept a copy.

face of the family drama he was witnessing before his own eyes. Moreover, he received death threats and strange phone calls, one in particular, around Christmas 1980, asking him if he were 'ready to receive three members of the Red Brigades'.* Remember, Soizic, how he finishes his conversations with you in *The Other Man*: 'A writer's old age can be very strange. Sometimes it's like his books: Evelyn Waugh, who had made such fun of Apthorpe's "thunder-box", died in the WC. Zola, like the miners in *Germinal*, was suffocated by charcoal fumes, and now, at the age of seventy-six, I find myself at grips with the criminal "*milieu*" of Nice – but I hope that I, at any rate, shall get the better of Pinkie.'

I want to stress three things: Graham was a direct witness of that entire affair; he was perfectly conscious of the risks he was taking; those who have read the pamphlet will have noted the words: 'Certainly there exists a Supreme Court in which one can have full confidence, but just as we have found everything blackened and blocked locally, we now discover the same obscure forces working away to prevent justice being done elsewhere.'

In the end we did get the better of Pinkie and justice was done. Graham had been so cross at the way the affair seemed to be turning out that he offered to resign as a Chevalier de la Légion d'Honneur and to return his insignia, so that he could 'feel at full liberty to speak out on behalf of the victims'.† At the same time, he sent a copy of the letter to Alain Peyrefitte, then Garde des Sceaux (minister of justice), stating the reasons for his resignation (which was considered not feasible). Graham thought that justice did not function in France. Mr Peyrefitte's reaction was immediate: he dispatched a judiciary inspector to the Riviera. The inspector's findings remain secret, but positive effects were clearly noticeable eventually.

* Letter dated 25 January 1982, *Yours etc.*
† Letter dated 22 December 1980, *Yours etc.*

Soizic: Did justice and morality have to be linked to the fates of people whom Graham helped, or did he sometimes help people for no particular reason, without any connection with a particular cause?

Yvonne: Of course. Graham could sometimes seem very reserved and distant to some people, but he was generous, as I've told you. A revealing anecdote comes to mind. Two hitchhikers who had nowhere to sleep knocked at his door one day (or at the entrance to the block of flats in Antibes, I don't know). Well, believe it or not, they looked so lost and broke – quite apart from the fact that he told me they were pleasant – that he put them up for the night. And you know how small his apartment was!

Soizic: What was his attitude, incidentally, to giving?

Yvonne: I never saw him regret doing so. He didn't expect anything in return. All the more so when it was a case of spontaneous gestures, such as when he came across beggars in the street or coming out of mass, for example. Once, however – it was a Sunday in Antibes – I saw him looking terribly morose. He had gone to the service on his own. 'What's the matter?' I asked. He replied in a gloomy voice: 'I think I've killed a man.' My heart skipped a beat. 'You know the beggar outside the church,' he said, 'the one I often give a small tip to? Well, today he wasn't there.' 'And so?' I said, somewhat relieved and beginning to see what he was talking about. 'Last Sunday, I don't know what came over me, but I felt I wanted to give him a large denomination note. Five hundred francs. And so I think that must have killed him,' said Graham, bursting into laughter.

In fact, he was very generous with his time, too, and in every way. A true pelican. He would have helped the worst of bandits if he felt that his human dignity had been insulted. For example, he was sorry for Jacques Mesrine, the famous gangster, whose tragic end moved him in spite of everything.* In short, he was a 'giver'. He fought against injustice, in a general way, and particularly against that feeling of power that money imparts. He illustrated this well in his book *Dr Fischer of Geneva* (1980).

Soizic: Did he have a particular person in mind? For you were living during the difficult period you have just described, and in the novel, too, money and corruption are closely linked.

Yvonne: I asked him that question, actually, and he replied in the negative. But it's nevertheless astonishing, with hindsight, that it's the only book whose subject is money.

Soizic: Aren't there touches of it in *The Captain and the Enemy*?

Yvonne: Anna-Luisa is certainly facing financial problems, and she plays 'dirty tricks' on the Captain so that he will help her bring up little Jim, but it's not the guiding theme of the book. Those two books are almost the antithesis of each other: money in the service of corruption; money as a support for love . . .

Soizic: In fact, didn't Graham also fight against the feeling of powerlessness that a lack of money brings?

Yvonne: Oh no! If someone had no money, he would have given him some. In my *Carnet rouge*, he said, 'I should not have liked to be a rich man. I like to feel the need to work in order to provide for my family.' Certainly, he wasn't poor. But he paid

---

* Jacques Mesrine (1939–79); shot by the police in November 1979, in Paris. See *L'Autre et son double* (Paris: Belfond, 1981, p. 234), omitted in the English edition, *The Other Man*: 'Occasionally, I have a weakness for certain "scoundrels". I couldn't help feeling rather shocked by Mesrine's death and the way the media "offered" him to a public that was already eager for the blood of those who are presented to them as "public enemies". '

himself monthly in some sort of way, so that his wealth went to his loved ones during his lifetime. In that way he rid himself of the burden of managing money – this was, of course, towards the end of his life. And to such an extent that, when there was a hitch, he didn't know how much he spent on everyday things. When he began to be seriously ill and needed nursing at home, at Châno, he told me he was worried about the cost of all the care, which may seem absurd, given who he was . . . He even got in touch with Jean-Félix Paschoud, a lawyer and his financial adviser. I can still hear him saying, 'Give me a global figure of what I have, for goodness' sake.' And when Jean-Félix gave him the figure, Graham's incredulous reaction was: 'But Jean-Félix, you're joking!' You see? And to think that he felt guilty, what's more, as far as his family was concerned, that he wasn't doing enough!

Soizic: Because what spurred him and made his blood boil, until the end of his life, was the question of human rights, in the most general meaning of the term, obviously.

Yvonne: Yes. His keen sense of responsibility stretched far beyond the family circle. Let's leave it to the biographers to draw up the list of royalties that were donated to such and such a cause, or such and such a monastery, or to victims of disasters. To the end, he was affected by sincere and genuine bursts of sympathy. It's not for me to mention them. But the opposite side to his moods of anger and indignation was this powerful capacity to take up the cause of those who had meant something to him. And he carried things through. Always. A gift for sympathy.

13

The Baffling Edge of Espionage

Where Graham Greene is concerned, one never seems to be able to escape from espionage, the doubts and questions it raises, the 'human factor' it sometimes strengthens – and Greene would agree here – between those who do not necessarily thrive on deception, but instead exert what one French writer has called '*un métier de seigneur*'.

Espionage was present in a sense at Greene's hospital bedside right up to the very last moments of his life. In Norman Sherry's letter of 28 March 1991 the interrogation was pressing and abrupt. 'Dear Graham, can I discuss Kim Philby with you?' he began, and the letter ended: 'I wish you felt you could write me last thoughts about Kim Philby and maybe also Yvonne who would have her own response to Kim Philby. But maybe you don't want me to see anything just yet. Perhaps you could leave some document for me to be read later. Love, Norman.' Sherry's entreaty had been lingering for more than a decade. That was his last letter to Graham.

In October 1990, only a few months before his death, Graham's concerns were focused on the fate of another friend whom he admiringly called 'a professional in the world of espionage'. I was in Antibes when, to my surprise, Graham handed me a brown envelope containing all the documents he had kept concerning Yves Allain, my father, who had been mysteriously assassinated in Morocco twenty-five years earlier. He had also sent me from Switzerland a long letter, dated 1 January 1991, which sheds an intriguing light on what the writer Greene knew – or did not know – about the 'dangerous edge of things'.

What Yvonne told me about Greene and espionage is complex and precious: encounters with Philby in Moscow (she was there; in fact, in a letter dated 22 December 1987, which I have seen, to his nephew James Greene, Graham wrote, 'One day you must hear about it all from Yvonne, who describes things much better than I do, and remembers more'); the atmosphere on the Riviera, where Graham often met pals from 'the old firm'; hints about his activities in Indochina, etc.

All these elements may help us towards an understanding of Greene the writer and the many men within. Yet the last moments I spent with Yvonne in August 2001, when she at last decided to speak out – albeit very sparingly – suddenly deepen the shadows surrounding Graham's 'divided loyalties'. They also cast a new light on Yvonne's own personality and confirm her previous assertion: 'My whole life has been a secret.' Which it was – almost to the end.

This chapter is presented as it was originally planned, though I have added the final brief insights into what Yvonne tells us as she slowly releases her 'secrets' and interrogations.

Soizic: In that kind of world one cannot fail to have doubts.

Yvonne: You're always forced to insert a question mark, and the question mark remains. You can have private convictions, and you can see what emerges over a lifetime – Graham's, for example – but you can't be a hundred per cent sure.

Soizic: If this secret service world still existed for Graham at the end of his life, whether occasionally or merely by chance, you were not in a good position to know, for the last person he would have spoken to about it was you. So you don't know anything, do you?

Yvonne: No. I'm sure that your mother, for example, had no inkling of what your father was doing at the time that he was . . .

Soizic: You told me you were prepared to admit – were you to be given proof – that Graham lied as far as these matters were concerned.

Yvonne: Indeed, and to accept it. I would understand him.

Soizic: Are there things to guide you today along that track? Can you envisage the possibility that Graham could have led different lives without your knowing it? Perhaps you have doubts . . .?

Yvonne: No, no, I have no doubts. It's just that if I were shown evidence that he had lied, well . . . But that would surprise me, because it wasn't in his temperament or his character. It would not tally with the person I knew, or how I remember him, or what I saw myself. If proof came to light one day, however, I should be forced to accept the facts.

Soizic: Isn't what is emerging from the various biographies and studies about Philby and Graham the beginnings of proof?

Yvonne: No, not for me. It's nothing but sensation. It's obvious that Philby will always sell.

Soizic: Did Graham ever lie at times, even about little things?

Yvonne: Never. There was of course a period in his life, at the time of the break-up with Dorothy and the beginning of the affair with Catherine, when he was obliged to lie, for Dorothy's peace of mind, particularly. But it pained him deeply. It was dreadful for him, and when, eventually, the truth came out, he felt so relieved because he hated having had to lie to three women at the same time: Vivien, at that difficult period, had not let go and hoped he would return to the fold; Dorothy knew about Catherine and made terrible scenes; and Catherine thought it was all a bit much, you see. Lying did not simplify his life! Afterwards, for even the slightest thing, he would say, 'Goodness, I've eaten an apple; but . . . no, it wasn't an apple, it was an orange.' Every tiny detail had to be absolutely accurate.

Soizic: Being accurate over details doesn't mean you aren't lying.

Yvonne: I agree. Let's say that it corresponded to a need in him: to establish the truth in its pure form. Even for an unimportant fib.

Soizic: People can also lie through omission or convenience.

Yvonne: No, not him. In thirty years I never caught him red-handed. He was not a man who lied. As proof of this I should like to mention his trip to Capri with Catherine in 1965. He could have said nothing to me: I had not been there yet, and there was no danger of repercussions. Yet he told me about it beforehand.

Soizic: Would you say he was an honest man?

Yvonne: You know, the word 'honest' has so many different meanings. Honest and good with other people, yes; honest with himself, I'm not entirely sure.

Soizic: Were his doubts about himself sincere?

Yvonne: Yes, certainly. But they weren't justified. He was too hard on himself. Towards other people he was always ready to be indulgent and forgive them.

Soizic: He wasn't a cheat?

Yvonne: No, no. A many-sided character, for sure, but not a cheat. During one period of his life, of course, he had to cheat – unwillingly, I would say – for the sake of others.

Soizic: You mean in his role as a secret agent during the war?

Yvonne: No, I was thinking of his relationships with women.

Soizic: As regards cheating or different degrees of reality, how could he reconcile the Catholic faith with visiting the brothels of Havana? Not that he was the only one!

Yvonne: He was a complex man, who seemed to have different compartments in his head. He could devote himself completely to religion and yet also delve into the mystery of a brothel in Cuba in all its shady aspects. There's a link to be made with his fascination for espionage. He always saw a connection between brothels and spying: when he was sent to Africa by MI6 during the war, he had had the idea of opening a 'house' where prostitutes would have been agents. He often said to me, 'Don't think that I went to brothels to do what other men normally do in those places. Firstly, I was intrigued. I wanted to know why those girls had come there. Furthermore, I found their conversations much more interesting than those one heard in fashionable circles.' He even kept up a correspondence with some of them.

Graham's secret was his passion for secrecy. Just as he was interested in priests and the power that confession conferred on them: so many secrets to unravel!

Soizic: He often said he would have made an excellent priest or a bad spy, because he forgot what he was told the moment he heard it. He told me in 1980: 'I don't think I could have seriously performed the role of double agent. But I feel a certain sympathy towards them. Philby must have felt that.'* And you

* *Oxford, 1919–1939* (Paris: Autrement, 1991), in which I make use of certain passages of a 1980 unpublished interview. M.-F.A.

once said, Yvonne, that even priests confided in him, particularly after *The Heart of the Matter* came out.

Don't all these remarks form part of a clever act? Didn't Graham play a game, particularly where Kim Philby was concerned? Various theses have been advanced lately, notably by Ronnie Challoner, a former member of the British secret service and an acquaintance of Graham's on the Côte d'Azur, which put forward a new scenario in which Kim was not simply a double but a triple agent, Graham being used as a privileged contact (without necessarily knowing it) so that certain information could be passed to the British Secret Service. The friendship between him and Philby was therefore secondary to the exigencies of Intelligence . . . The consequences such a hypothesis would have had for Graham were made (but not attributed) by Ron Rosenbaum in the *New York Times Magazine* of 10 July 1994: 'It would mean that Philby had been laughing at Greene.' A priori, this appears too much, of course, but what do you think about it?

Yvonne: Oh, come on, all this is so spicy! I can only repeat what I was told by Rufina, Kim's wife, who actually came here, to Switzerland – and I also talked to her when I went back to the Soviet Union in September 1991. She said, 'To suggest that Kim became a triple agent after he came to Moscow is pure nonsense.'

Soizic: But then what do wives know about men like that? She would have been kept out of it, in any case.

Yvonne: In her case, it's absolutely unthinkable, and I really believe that. From what I saw of Kim Philby, he wasn't going to begin another career over there. His physical state, his health and his age did not allow him to question everything and put his

life at risk. As Graham said when he returned from the shores of the Suez Canal after the Six-Day War, 'I'm too old now to be killed like that far from home.' It was the same for Kim Philby.

There are limits. I think he really didn't want to do anything else. I could be wrong, of course, but that's my deep-down intuition. What's more, and it's one of the qualities Graham recognised in him, what he did he did out of conviction and not for money, even if he did have a good pension and live in a well-appointed flat. Besides, in real espionage it's not the money that matters. Everything that has been written about this has been bluff, hot air, or done – yes – for money. Money didn't interest Kim Philby.

Soizic: Do you think he was still working for the KGB or that they used him from time to time as a consultant?

Yvonne: As a consultant.

Soizic: He'd been put out to grass, in short. You told me that when you saw him in Moscow you had the feeling that he was a finished man.

Yvonne: Certainly not a triple agent who had begun a bright new career out there, no!

Soizic: And was that Graham's impression too?

Yvonne: We didn't talk about it.

Soizic: Did Graham ever mention the theory that Philby might be a triple agent?

Yvonne: No, never, because it didn't occur to him. For him, Kim Philby's real career came to an end in 1963, when he left Beirut for Moscow. And Norman Sherry never had an answer from Graham on the matter, whatever certain newspapers may have insinuated or said. Neither was it possible for Norman's letter of 28 March 1991, which I possess, to have been discovered beside Graham's bed at the hospital a week after

Yvonne Cloetta in the mid-1960s.
Courtesy Joan Reinhardt

Lunch in Antibes, 1989.
© J.B.Diederich/ CONTACT Press Images

Berkhamsted Collegiate School.
Courtesy Berkhamsted
Collegiate School

**Greene with his
sister Elisabeth and
brother Hugh, 1983.**
© Amanda Saunders

**Greene with his nieces
Amanda Saunders and
Louise Dennys, 1979.**
Courtesy Amanda
Saunders

Lunch with Charlie Chaplin (*second from right*), a close friend of Greene's.
Courtesy Joan Reinhardt

Old friends: Greene's
publisher Max and his wife
Joan Reinhardt.
Courtesy Joan Reinhardt

Greene having breakfast in his flat in Antibes.
Private Collection

Yvonne Cloetta with Kim Philby's wife, Rufa Philby (*left*)
and Greene's Russian translator.
© Ruth Lazarus

Kim Philby, the third man.
© Getty images

Yvonne and Greene on their last
trip to Russia in 1986.
Courtesy Amanda Saunders

Yvonne at Greene's grave at the
cemetery in Corseaux.
© Ruth Lazarus

Yvonne Cloetta in the mid-1990's
Courtesy Brigitte Cloetta-Lehner

his death, giving credence to the notion that Graham had had some revelation to make. It's absurd! But Graham was worried when he received the letter; of course he was. He admitted to me, 'I'm anxious about what Norman has to say about this affair . . . God knows what Norman is going to say.' Caroline, Graham's daughter, told me about Norman's endeavours: a week after Graham's death, she went to the Providence hospital with him. He was determined to get into Graham's room. Naturally, he was not allowed in. He said he wanted to take photographs of his bed. He was unsuccessful.

I believe Norman did all this to obscure the mystery of Philby and Greene, and to stir up the flames, do you see?

No, Philby's real career was over. I learnt later – not from Philby directly, but from interviews Kim gave to Phillip Knightley – about the way he was treated in Moscow at the beginning. It was such a disappointment to him. After all his struggles on their behalf, he expected to be greeted as a hero by the Soviets – the KGB, in particular. That was far from the case. After the battlefield, it was the desert crossing. The object of mistrust and suspicion, he felt in some way rejected by his own. He started to drink – drink as if he were suicidal. He wanted to destroy himself. It was Rufa who rescued him. She told me this when she came to visit me. And yet we should remember what Kim surprisingly said to us in Moscow in 1986: 'The evening of my life is golden.' Moreover, his old dream had even come true for him, as he had once expressed it: 'To have Graham Greene opposite me, and a bottle of wine on a table between us.'

Soizic: Could all this perhaps have been a set-up, to confuse the issue?

Yvonne: Hardly. Not during the Brezhnev period! Once he was in Moscow, he couldn't even be a 'double' any longer. Besides, Philby disliked the term 'double agent'. For instance, at one of our meetings, at the Georgian restaurant Aragvi, in Moscow in

September 1987, when the conversation turned to 'what we'd do if we had our chance again' etc., he suddenly said angrily, 'I'm always treated as a spy or a traitor. But a traitor to what and to whom? I've never belonged to the establishment. It was up to them to know what I was doing. I never betrayed my true friends, the Russians. The right I have done is greater than the wrong I have done.' You see? That's what Graham told you: 'Philby really lived out his loyalty.'*

But I have to admit that, as far as I'm concerned, there was nevertheless Kim the friend and Kim the spy. He had that gentle, hypocritical expression – he looked like the perfect spy.

Soizic: Should we forget some of the dreadful deeds he was responsible for?

Yvonne: Ah, but you'd have fallen for his charm, despite everything. And yet when I knew him, in 1986, he was no longer young; just some years younger than Graham. Eight, in fact. He suffered from emphysema and he was very ill. But he was a delightful man. I'm sorry to have to tell you that. He had extraordinary charm. He needed it for the job he was doing. He took everyone in. Physically, he was nothing special: he wasn't handsome, and only average height, but as soon as he started speaking, his expression and his smile melted you.

Soizic: Do you think Graham may have fallen for that charm?

Yvonne: No

Soizic: What was it, then?

Yvonne: They used to meet during the war, in the evenings in London during the Blitz, at a restaurant, and for Graham (who

* *The Other Man*, p. 20.

never stopped making a mockery of the Secret Service afterwards) at that time, joining the Secret Service was a great adventure.

Soizic: This basis for their friendship is confirmed by a letter Graham wrote to me, on 1 January 1991, in reply to one of mine: 'You ask me why I liked Kim Philby so much: I had grown to appreciate him immensely during the period I had been working with him.' And he added, 'And later, after he left, he wrote to me from Moscow to support a request I had made. I was asking for my books not to be published in Russia.' The letter was surprisingly discursive, for it expanded on their correspondence and their political vision of the war in Afghanistan, almost as if, in retrospect, Graham wanted to exonerate Philby and the intelligence branch of the KGB of the period.

Soizic: Did Graham suspect the double game he was playing, in 1943 or later? He said to me in 1980, 'When the war was over, Philby was on a different side. Naturally, when I knew him, we and the Russians were fighting the same enemy.' To the question 'Was it a comfort to you not to have been aware of his activities as a double agent?' he replied, 'I didn't know anything then. All I knew was that Philby, like me, was a man of the left . . . It was only much later, of course, that I realised that he wasn't working for his own ends. I could only respect him the more. He was playing a very dangerous game. He was very brave.'*

Yvonne: Whether he suspected his activities or not, when I asked him the question, he replied with a firm 'No'. For him Philby was a charismatic boss who had 'all the small loyalties to his colleagues, and, of course, his big loyalty was unknown to us'.† On the other hand, Graham never mentioned anything to me about it.

* *Oxford, 1919–1939*, op. cit, p. 34.
† Graham Greene, Introduction, Kim Philby, *My Silent War* (London, MacGibbon and Kee Ltd, 1968). (The book was not published until 1980 in the Soviet Union.)

Certainly Graham, after Burgess and Maclean fled to Moscow, had no further doubts about Kim.

Soizic: So he knew immediately – or had always known – that Philby was the 'third man'?

Yvonne: Not necessarily, no; he hadn't always known. But when the two of them left, it caused quite a commotion. Bear in mind that Graham was not the only one to have understood what was going on. And for a very good reason, because they all worked in the same section. He had realised Kim was involved.

Soizic: It seems to have strengthened his admiration for him: 'He was a major player,' he also told me in 1980. 'The secret service is often filled with incompetent nobodies. At the time, the only section that was working well was that managed by Kim Philby. He would probably have become head of the Secret Service if Burgess and Maclean hadn't fled. It was in this sense that he was a very important double agent.' His defection didn't seem to damage their friendship, did it?

Yvonne: No, on the contrary. I must make it clear that Kim's revelations in 1963, after his truncated confessions and his flight to Beirut, had a tidal-wave effect on Graham. But on a positive level they shed new light on Kim's behaviour in 1944, and for that very reason revived a friendship between them that had been deeply shaken. And yet between 1963 and 1986 they never met. They corresponded: twelve letters and a postcard from Cuba, from Kim. Nine letters from Graham. I kept photocopies.

Soizic: Why so long before their reunion?

Yvonne: Because Graham's 'quarrel' with his Soviet friends over the Daniel and Sinyavsky affair had intervened. They had been accused of having their books, which were banned in the

USSR, published in the West. So a long separation had to follow.

Soizic: Can you try to describe their friendship?

Yvonne: Throughout the time I saw Graham and Kim together in Moscow, when they had not seen each other for so many years, I said to myself, 'If they're friends, they must have certain essential ideas in common.' I had seen what Graham thought of the regime, and that he disapproved of it completely, as he demonstrated on several occasions. And I wondered how Kim, who had to live in Moscow, and was really trapped there, could endure it.

Soizic: Didn't they have more or less the same ideas or illusions about Communism? In *The Other Man* Graham quoted George Orwell, who described him as 'the Catholic fellow-traveller'.

Yvonne: No. You have to distinguish between the two men, if only because of the difference in the intensity of their idealism and their convictions. Philby went to the very end. Graham's interest very soon waned. The story about his becoming a member of the Communist Party for four weeks in Oxford in 1923 was simply so that he could make a trip to Russia. Whereas with Philby it was really deep-rooted. Graham was far less idealistic than him and he lost his enthusiasm once he realised that life in the Soviet Union did not quite correspond with the idea he had of it from Marxist theories.

Soizic: When was that? He told me about four journeys he made to the Soviet Union during the Gorbachev period.

Yvonne: When he went there with his son in 1957, then in 1961, I think, which was the last time before 1986. No, between Graham and Philby, it really was the 'human factor', even if it wasn't easy to deal with, considering the pressure coming from Britain on the part of the public, not to mention the possible moral repercussions on the two individuals. So if there was one man for whom Graham committed himself totally, it was Kim Philby. And he really had to be fond of him to do that. The first meetings between them actually date from 1941. Graham was finishing his military training; Kim at the time was head of a small section of the Intelligence Service dealing with German and Italian activities in Portugal and West Africa, including Sierra Leone (which Graham knew already), where he was posted. After a gap of about two years, they found themselves in the same section, the SIS, under Philby's command, as he told you. In June 1944, Graham turned down Kim's offer of promotion and decided to stop all official activities in the Intelligence Service. Incidentally, I can tell you that he'd had enough, because this petty bureaucrat work did not correspond at all with the image he had of the Secret Service.

Soizic: Indeed, Graham told me in 1980, 'In *The Human Factor* I wanted to describe that dreary routine, so unlike John le Carré's or James Bond's.'*

Yvonne: Besides, he had already decided to devote himself to writing. He couldn't do both.

Soizic: So you don't think Graham left because he had a premonition about Philby's role?

Yvonne: No, no. Of course, I can only go by what he told me and by my own personal experience of what happened. Nevertheless, the real causes of their break-up in 1944 remain obscure and their subsequent statements differ noticeably: according to Kim, it was purely his refusal to compromise a friend that explained the decision; according to Graham, the retraction of a friend whose motives seemed to him guided by personal

* Unpublished conversation with M.-F.A., 1980.

ambition inevitably led to a break-up. Later, he would write about this in his introduction to Kim's book *My Silent War*: 'I am glad now that I was wrong. He was serving a cause and not himself, and now my old liking for him comes back . . .'

Soizic: Was it because of Kim the friend or Kim the spy?

Yvonne: Graham never allowed himself to be taken in by the 'seductiveness' of espionage. His friendship with Kim was to do with the man he was, not because he was a spy. Kim had a fine sense of humour, which Graham appreciated. What is certain is that for him Kim enshrined one of the great problems of his age. They had common interests. Graham confessed to me one day: 'I know, deep down, that what Kim wanted was to bring down the Nazis.' He suffered from the knowledge of their existence, just as anyone would. And in his 1991 letter to you he explained the roots of Kim's choice: 'Given the context, it was more natural, at the beginning of the 1930s, to take sides with our possible ally, Russia.'

So afterwards, as you know, Graham, acting purely on his own convictions, wrote that introduction to *My Silent War*. He risked compromising himself. He risked losing his credibility. And he really did stick his neck out. But his introduction really did protect Kim.

Some say that it cost him the Nobel Prize, but I don't believe that, because the story about the member of the jury who systematically opposed his nomination came before this.*

Soizic: You say Graham 'risked compromising himself'. So was there a risk?

* Yvonne explained that Arthur Lonquist, an influential member of the jury, reacted in a very hostile way to a performance of a play based on *The Power and the Glory* when it was performed at the Royal Theatre, Stockholm: 'A black flag should be flying over the Royal Theatre. The flag of the plague', he had written. And, according to Graham, he was obdurate.

Yvonne: Actually, no. His reasoning, as he confided to me at the time, was the opposite of that kind of logic, because in coming out openly as a defender of Kim Philby he proved that he knew nothing about all this.

Soizic: Where did Philby stand on the scale of friendship for Graham?

Yvonne: You wouldn't say Philby was his best friend, but he's the one he took most risks for. He's the most spectacular example of what Graham was able to do. And he never stopped speaking up for him, even to his friends in the 'old firm'. I frequently observed this. They would explode with rage and hatred. Graham attributed this purely and simply to the feelings of jealousy that footsoldiers have for an important general, and this was only increased by the fact that they knew Philby could have been 'C'. When Kim died, someone wrote in an English newspaper, 'I hope he died in agony.' Graham, who was saddened by his friend's death, was shocked and furious. He said to me, 'Those people do more harm than anything Kim Philby could have done.' As to his colleagues and former colleagues on the Côte d'Azur, they, naturally, did not agree with Graham and could not understand his friendship with Philby, even if they retained a certain sympathy for the man himself, while disapproving utterly of his activities.

Soizic: I, too, have often wondered how Graham could have disregarded his activities.

Yvonne: He didn't disregard them. I remember we were having lunch one day with the British consul, Paul Paulson, and his wife. We met at L'Escargot, in Antibes. Since he had belonged to the 'old firm', the conversation turned naturally to Kim. Graham said, 'Please, let's stop. Here we are in a restaurant. We won't quarrel.' But Paul, who was sitting next to me, was concerned, because in an aside to me he whispered, 'Don't believe what Graham says, for he was very fond of Kim Philby, but he's been an awful man and he was responsible for the deaths of many people, in Albania especially, in 1949.' When we returned home, I told Graham this, for I kept no secrets from him. So he then told me the entire story from A to Z, explaining that it was a civil war and that, yes, it was true that those who had come ashore were dissidents; that there had been a great deal of damage caused by Kim's revealing secret knowledge; but that if the reverse had happened there would still, at the end of the day, have been Albanians killed.*

Soizic: It's not an argument. The dissidents had a very different notion of Albania from the one that had taken root during the communist era. So it's a very serious matter.

Yvonne: So you would have rejected Philby?

Soizic: I can't disregard forty-five years of dictatorship, or the Albanian camps, the survivors of which I saw in 1991. But it's a curious thing, that friendship, even when people know this or that . . .

Yvonne: Just as one cannot explain love, one cannot explain friendship either.

Soizic: And yet when he was asked what his reaction would have been had he known what Philby was up to when Graham was working for him, he said, 'I would have given him twenty-four hours to get away, then I'd have reported him to the Services.' So there were limits to his friendship, weren't there?

* cf. Norman Sherry, *Graham Greene*, vol. 2, p. 489: 'They were going into their country, armed to do damage to that country. They were killed instead of killing.'

Yvonne: Graham's loyalty was unshakeable. To a friend.

Soizic: Wasn't he drawn a little too far?

Yvonne: They both stayed alive.

Soizic: What do you mean? Aren't you yourself opening the door to all sorts of hypotheses?

Yvonne: I jotted down his words: 'Sharing a feeling of doubt can bring men together even more than sharing a faith . . .'

Soizic: Do you think it was this that drew Philby and Graham to each other, at the end of the day? I'm thinking of their correspondence about Afghanistan. Could Philby have been a sort of dissident? Did you have the impression that when they met they were tacitly putting on an act?

Yvonne: If Graham was putting on an act with Kim Philby, he was putting on a very good one. A terrific one! Because there was nothing in his behaviour – really nothing – throughout all those years that could have allowed me to think that he was playing a double game, or that he was lying or telling me stories. Absolutely nothing. Or else they were both excellent actors – which was not something that would have surprised me about Kim Philby, but it didn't apply to Graham. And even when you have a marvellous actor, there's always some little thing that gives him away . . . No, quite simply they were two companions meeting after not seeing each other for a long time.

Soizic: And who observed one another?

Yvonne: No, they didn't observe one another.

Soizic: Was it Philby who had asked to see Graham?

Yvonne: Yes. Before this trip, Graham said to me, 'As I'm going there, I should like to meet my friend Kim.' When I asked, 'Why do you want to see him again?' he replied, 'Firstly because he's a friend, and it's always pleasant to meet a friend you haven't seen for a very long time; and then, out of curiosity, too. I should like to see how much he has remained an Englishman and how Russian he's become.' That was typical of Graham. All of which leads one to think that he hadn't met him on previous visits. On this first trip to the Soviet Union, we went first of all to Moscow, then to Leningrad, and afterwards to Georgia. It was only on our return that a meeting with Philby was arranged. Naively, I'd said to Graham, 'Why don't you telephone him?' 'No, he knows I'm here, and if he wants to see me he'll make the first move. I'll leave him alone; I'll let him come to me. I won't do a thing.' Eventually, we were asked to dinner with Philby and his wife.

Soizic: Were there four of you?

Yvonne: Yes, but to begin with there was also the secretary-general of the Writers' Union, Henrick Borovick, a well-known journalist, who had accompanied us. It was clear that precautions had been taken. The driver didn't drop us at the building where the Philbys lived, he asked us to get out just before we got there; Rufa came to meet us at a given point, in a small street behind where he lived . . . Henrick came too. We had an aperitif together, and then he left and the four of us ate together. Well, my eyes were on stalks from the very beginning, as you can imagine. First of all, they just stared wide-eyed at one another, and then, when Kim was able to speak, he said, 'Well, it's obvious that a lot of water has flowed by: you're looking a good deal older.' Graham: 'No more than you.' You don't really think they could have been putting on an act . . . Several seconds passed before they could speak to one another. It was quite obvious there was a lot of emotion there. Then, when they did speak, it was in English, of course.

Soizic: Had Kim Philby become slightly Russian?

Yvonne: No. Totally English. One hundred per cent.

Soizic: Did you have the impression that he was being watched? That it was as if he was in prison?

Yvonne: No, not in prison, but . . . he was living in a flat which belonged to the KGB, and when we met the following day, at the restaurant, he had a car – but one with curtains. I would say not so much watched as protected. One tiny detail I did notice – you'll find it in Kim's letters to Graham – he spoke a great deal about his mother-in-law, Rufa's mother, whom he was very fond of, by the way. And he said that she was very worried about him, and he didn't know why. Well, it so happened that at a particular moment, while we were still having our aperitif, I went into the kitchen to talk to Rufa, who was cooking dinner. She said, 'The telephone is bound to ring, and it's bound to be my mother, because she knows someone is coming to dinner tonight. She's going to telephone to find out how everything was going, how it all went.' And, sure enough, the telephone did ring. So was it her mother, or someone else?

Soizic: Did they try to assassinate Philby?

Yvonne: Not as far as I know.

Soizic: And Graham?

Yvonne: No.

Soizic: Because what strikes me about Graham, as far as the 'deadly zones' of politics and espionage are concerned, notably in the Prologue and Dedication to *The Other Man*, is his setting the record straight: 'It's a world where I've never been anything but a minor cog, an amateur for a few years during the war.' He seems to be expressing his admiration for those 'more important' than him, but also for the danger inherent in spying – which you suggested spontaneously just now. You stressed that with Philby Graham had immediately taken certain precautions. But don't you think the opening up of the Thatcher–Gorbachev talks and the beginnings of perestroika may have encouraged one side or the other to try to make overtures, with Philby or Graham used as intermediaries, for example?

Yvonne: I don't know. The overall atmosphere of their meeting was cautious, even so. Philby's first words to Graham were: 'Please, Graham, don't ask me any questions about the past.' To begin with, I was not allowed to ask any questions whatsoever.

Soizic: So their conversation was actually rather banal, in fact.

Yvonne: Yes, Graham asked questions about his life in Moscow. As for me, I couldn't resist. I said, 'Kim, may I be allowed to ask you a question?' He replied: 'Go on, then.' 'What do you think of General de Gaulle?' I wanted to see whether, by asking obliquely about de Gaulle . . . He replied: 'Naturally, he's a man whom I admire very much. I greatly admired him as a military leader, but naturally his political views afterwards . . .' There was nothing more to be got out of him, you see.

When we met again the next day as guests of the Borovicks, Kim arrived looking very tired.

Soizic: He'd probably had to endure an interrogation or an informative conversation?

Yvonne: No, no. I said, 'You're really tired, Kim.' He answered, 'Of course I'm tired. By five o'clock in the morning I still hadn't slept a wink.' I asked, 'Why? Weren't you feeling well?' (I was deliberately playing the fool, you see.) Looking distressed, he explained, 'No, when I'd met a friend, a friend like Graham, whom I hadn't seen for over twenty years, how could I possibly sleep? I didn't want to in the least, for it would have been time lost.' So, you see, the heartless man he has been portrayed as – obviously I'm not saying that you don't have to have nerves of steel to do what he did – was nevertheless capable of feeling. It's not something you make up. And I really did have the impression that the two men were meeting like friends who did not want to hark back to the past any more, and especially that Graham should not ask him questions about what he had actually done.

As far as I know, Graham never confronted Philby face to face.

Soizic: Do you think Graham was fascinated by disloyalty, or was he actually appalled by it?

Yvonne: That's a very difficult question. He didn't speak in those terms. When he spoke of Philby, he was careful not to make judgements about what he did. He used to say that he went as far as his convictions allowed.

Soizic: I was talking about disloyalty as a constant feature of his work. Did he confront disloyalty head on? It may be the case that, if he did remain friends with an 'official traitor' like Philby, this wasn't something that particularly appalled him. And yet it gave him grounds for anxiety, didn't it?

Yvonne: Yes, but it was much more to do with betraying a person. He made a crucial distinction here. He always used to say, 'Who among us has not committed treason to something or someone more important than a country?'* It's the story of Sarah and Maurice Castle in *The Human Factor*. Love is a 'total risk', but they don't betray each other. They are betrayed by the various Services.

* Introduction to *My Silent War*.

Soizic: Wasn't Graham in some ways close to thinking that it was Philby who had been betrayed? Why was there this similarity between *The Human Factor* and Philby's story?

Yvonne: This similarity was a pure coincidence – and I was witness to what happened when he discovered the first pages of the manuscript. It was in 1970, during the winter. It was cold in the flat, but not so cold that it was necessary to turn on the central heating. He kept two small electric radiators there. I took a step-ladder and went into the bedroom to look on top of the cupboards where the radiators were kept. Then I said, 'What's that there behind them?' 'What do you mean?' he asked. 'There's a whole pile of papers here,' I replied. 'Well, can you bring them down?' I started to pull out the papers and handed them to him. What were they? Well, he had a vague memory of some pages that he had completely forgotten from *The Tenth Man*. He thought it was only the synopsis. In fact, he discovered the entire manuscript. At the same time, he came across a few pages – but not more than a dozen in this case – of a manuscript he had begun over ten years earlier and which he had entitled *The Human Factor*! He had started to write it in 1959–60 (originally with the title *The Cold Fault*), but he had abandoned it because in 1963 Kim disappeared and he said to himself that everyone would think that he just wanted to retell the story of Philby. So he put it aside. When we discovered these pages of manuscript, he read them again and said: 'Well, now that this affair is over, I may be able to carry on with my research.' He thought that these dozen or so pages were good and could lead to something interesting.

Soizic: So he had begun the book before Philby escaped to Moscow?

Yvonne: That's right. Before Kim had defected.

Soizic: So you can see the conclusions that might be drawn. That in fact he hadn't wanted to publish it at the time, either because his writer's intuition had helped him figure out what Philby was up to, and he didn't want anyone to suspect that he, Graham, had been in the know; or else that he didn't want to betray a friend by giving food for thought to readers and the press.

Yvonne: No, no, those hypotheses are childish. It's actually a disease, this business of people wanting to involve themselves systematically in other people's secrets – secrets they don't want to disclose. I must say I don't like it when people involve themselves in mine, either.

Soizic: Fine, I won't go on. Is it true that Philby balked slightly, when Graham sent him his manuscript, at certain passages which, according to him, put undue stress on the sinister and ugly atmosphere of Moscow at that time?

Yvonne: Yes. In his reply to Kim of 17 May 1978, Graham apologised: 'I am sorry if I made Moscow too bleak.' But, even so, he didn't revise his text.

Soizic: The letter Graham sent me on 1 January 1991 certainly brought with it a very serious message as far as my family was concerned. On the subject of my father's fate, he wrote, 'I still think that the roots of the matter might be turned up in Czechoslovakia,' and he ended like this, almost as if I should draw a lesson from it: 'As you may have read in my speech in Hamburg published under the title "The Virtue of Disloyalty", I never believed in the prime importance of loyalty to one's country. Loyalty to individuals seems to me to be far more important.' In the brown envelope he had 'bequeathed' to me earlier in Antibes, there was nothing but press cuttings . . . Did Graham know something? Was he fantasising about it?*

Yvonne: Well, I have that brown envelope here. At least, copies of the papers Graham gave you at your last meeting.

Soizic: So you know very well that there's nothing very interesting inside, apart from press cuttings.

Yvonne: True. And yet throughout his life Graham wondered about your father's assassination. He even thought of basing a novel on it.

Soizic: But how, in this 1991 letter, which is a last message to me, could he be quite so positive?

Yvonne: It was the result of imagining all the possibilities and thinking about these questions over a long time.

Soizic: Precisely, and because he was involved in the espionage world, that bothers me. It sounds as if it was a trail . . . There's something mysterious about it, after all.

---

* After the publication of *The Other Man*, Graham Greene had strongly encouraged me to make enquiries about the Yves Allain 'affair'. He wanted me to write a book or a novel. He often rang up to spur me on: 'How is your book going?' he would say. I had in fact done some research and begun a book, but it drove me to despair and came to nothing. It was only when I was completing this chapter, some months after Yvonne's death, that I realised that Graham, in one of his last gestures of friendship, may simply have been urging me to take up my task again. All of a sudden, the last lines of his Prologue and Dedication to *The Other Man* came back to me. He wrote: 'and the long and possibly dangerous task of discovering the truth must fall to some younger writer.' [M.-F.A.]

Yvonne: There wasn't. I'm convinced there was no new element, no revelation. Because he would have told you himself. No, it was a personal intuition. So, you see, how can people maintain, as some do, that Graham actually did have some really deep-rooted connections in the East? At the time, he could have obtained certain responses from the East, but he would have told you. For the sake of friendship. Throughout his life, Graham tried to find a link. Because of your father . . . This tragic story confirms that Graham did not have access to the Secret Service.

Soizic: Or that he could not tell me anything about what he had hinted at in his letter. Perhaps to protect us . . . He only did so, what's more, when he knew he was very ill.

Yvonne: There was only one thing that made sense in Graham's case, and that was close affection.

Soizic: But what were those intuitions based on? How did Graham know about such things?

Yvonne: Because he had so many friends who were involved. Because of his own experience, too. During the war, and afterwards. In Indochina, for example.

Soizic: He told me he had played a sort of 'go-between' role 'on a mission to contact Ho Chi Minh in Hanoi, once the French had pulled out'.* On the flyleaf of the French translation of *The Quiet American*, the inscription to my parents (16 September 1959) reads: '. . . from Graham, the aged spy from Indo-China'. He inscribed your copy: '. . . from the unknown Graham'. Did he talk to you about this famous letter he had been asked to deliver to Ho Chi Minh? Graham never wanted to say

* *The Other Man*, p. 9.

much more than 'I'm not free to talk about it. All I can say is that I was asked to hand him a letter. The "mission" was carefully prepared. I even had to resort to a touch of blackmail.'* The description of his meeting follows. But, as he wrote in one of his essays, 'I had guaranteed that I would not publish the details of our conversation.'† He was scarcely more prolix in *Ways of Escape*, although he did provide a number of additional 'details'.‡

Yvonne: There is indeed a sort of secret or mystery there, because I've never known the contents of that letter either. Furthermore, Ho Chi Minh gave him a film, and that film has disappeared. Yes, disappeared. Graham never knew what became of it. He thought he had brought it back with him to England, and then he never found it again.

Soizic: He didn't know what it was about?

Yvonne: No. It was about the war. Graham was absolutely furious about it. He was annoyed with himself because he was convinced that he had mislaid it. He never suspected anyone of having stolen it. He said to me: 'Perhaps I lent it, or gave it to someone.' It's a mystery.

Soizic: Was Indochina the logical extension of his involvement in the Secret Service during the Second World War?

Yvonne: Graham would have responded in his usual elusive way that it was 'quite by chance' that he found himself there. But I know that Trevor Wilson, the British consul in Hanoi, with whom he had become very friendly since the war, persuaded him to go there, either directly or via his sister Elisabeth. You see, you can never get away from the world of espionage.

* *The Other Man*, ibid.
† Graham Greene, *Collected Essays* (London: Bodley Head, 1969), p. 402.
‡ *Ways of Escape* (London: Bodley Head, 1980), pp. 154–62.

He often spoke to me about Vietnam – or, I should say, Indochina. It was a part of his life he had enjoyed. Apart from his love for the country and its people, he also had some sympathy for the French.* General de Lattre knew and sensed that. At the same time, he was suspicious of Graham, and of his links with Trevor, particularly. He succeeded in having him sent back to London, what's more. In the end, an unsigned telegram (in fact, it was from Marie Biche, Graham's previous literary agent in France) wrecked everything: Marie told him that Dorothy Glover had decided to become a Catholic, instructed by the Jesuit priest Father Philip Caraman. The French Secret Service, who had intercepted the message, took it as a coded message: 'Your friend will arrive on Thursday. Dorothy under instruction from Philip.' This appeared to confirm them in their suspicions and they kept an eye on his every movement, as did de Lattre himself, who displayed a sort of contempt for 'this writer', as he referred to him.†

Soizic: Don't you get the feeling though, that espionage was a bit of a game for him? The story of the lost film doesn't sound very professional, does it? Or maybe Graham was just pulling your leg?

Yvonne: It appeared as if he was having fun, but that was merely appearance. *The Quiet American* illustrates his preoccupations, by the way. In it, according to what his friend Gloria Emerson told you, he was already exposing 'the murderous good intentions of the Americans', and his 'absolute determination to help the Vietnamese'.‡ And who knows what

* *The Other Man*, p. 111: 'I don't think that *The Quiet American* leaves any trace of my private ambivalence as between my pro-French and my pro-VietMinh sympathies . . . I must have expressed my doubts clearly enough to have had Marshal de Lattre accuse me once at dinner of being a spy . . .'
† *Ways of Escape*, op. cit. pp. 154–62.
‡ Cf. M.-F. Allain, '*L'Amérique serre les rangs autour de ses anciens du Vietnam*', *Le Monde diplomatique*, August 1986.

risks Graham took when he delivered that famous letter to Ho Chi Minh?*

Soizic: But it's also true that espionage was a subject that entertained him, isn't it?

Yvonne: Yes, he enjoyed mocking it and standing back from it somewhat. Particularly when he was with your father. In the flat in boulevard Malesherbes (we had invited your parents to dinner; this must have been in 1959 or shortly afterwards), they launched into the subject, as I mentioned earlier. They were like two small children and they spent the evening in fits of laughter. Graham loved playing pranks. Your father wasn't quite so keen, but he joined in that evening.

Soizic: During your years together, did he expect you to join in his jokes?

Yvonne: No, not really. Once he left England, all that was over. But the mood would still come over him. He liked to talk about them.

Soizic: He was still an adolescent at heart . . .

Yvonne: It's hard to say. On the one hand, he was so mature, so tormented. On the other, you couldn't say that he was still childish, but like all men he had a slightly puerile side. With his friends he may have felt the need to experience what he possibly missed in his childhood.

Soizic: Going back to the Old Spies Club, did he see much of former members of the 'old firm'?

* See Yvonne's clarification on the subject of Greene and Vietnam in a letter in 1995 to Alberto Huerta, a liberation theologian, who had corresponded with Graham.

Yvonne: Yes. There were several who lived in the south of France. They made up a sort of fraternity. They all looked as if they were playing at being spies!

Soizic: Who was there?

Yvonne: The former British consul in Nice, Paul Paulson, and Sir John Cairncross – whom I never met – were already there. Graham called Cairncross 'Claymore', he never knew why. But he was always 'Claymore'. He felt sorry that after so many years Cairncross should have had to endure all that bother, but he was prepared to admit that he could in fact have been the 'fifth man'. Or the 'sixth' – I'm no longer sure what they've come up with! Cairncross had belonged to the same section as him in MI6 – the Iberian section, I think. There was also Ronnie Challoner, who was particularly devoted to Graham, and who bought his flat in Antibes after his death. Ronnie was especially interested in the wealth of correspondence between the two men. When I telephoned Cairncross, according to Graham's wishes, after Graham's death, he simply told me to send back his letters by post . . . Popov, code-named 'Tricycle', also lived on the Côte d'Azur; he was a former Yugoslav agent who had worked for the American Secret Service, and who had warned them – without being taken seriously, alas – about the attack on Pearl Harbor. Graham went to see him several times, and I accompanied him on one or two occasions. We had been invited there by Lulu Goud. Popov was suffering from cancer of the spine. Graham greatly admired him. He felt the same admiration for Popov as he did for Philby.*

* cf. *The Other Man*, p. 184: 'In time of war, espionage is an essential weapon. Not far from me in the South of France lived one of the double agents who served our cause to great effect during the war. His name was Popov. He was Jugoslav. He was sent to England by the German secret service, but he was already working for us . . .'

All in all, Graham lived and breathed that atmosphere. It was a world he frequented. The greater majority of them were former SIS people, in France or in England, starting with his sister, because it was she who recruited him. Do you remember the dedication of *The Human Factor*? 'To my sister, Elisabeth Dennys, who cannot deny some responsibility.'

Soizic: Yvonne, do you think Graham could have been disloyal to Britain?

Yvonne: I often wonder how far Graham's attraction to the Russians extended, what explained that attraction . . . I often ponder what he told me – and wrote in the margins of my little *Carnet rouge* – after he met Gorbachev in February 1987.

I wasn't with him on that trip; he went alone. Then, back home, when we were discussing communism, he wrote, 'Today, thanks to Mr Gorbachev, things evolve quickly, and I am happy about that. Last month, at that forum on human rights in Moscow, I publicly declared to Gorbachev and the audience that my dream before I died was to see a Soviet ambassador posted to the Vatican, so he could provide the Pope with some pieces of good advice!' Then, on the other side of the page, his commentary runs on: 'Those of us who have shared the round tables – and very boring they were – met Gorbachev in a small room in the Kremlin, before the huge general meeting. To me as we shook hands, he said, "I have known you for some years, Mr Greene."'

He wrote that himself. Gorbachev spoke in English, without an interpreter. Gorbachev's remark is quite enigmatic. Of course, Graham was famous as a writer, and that was a compliment Gorbachev was paying him, but I wonder . . . Wasn't Graham leaving a clue in my *Carnet rouge*?

That's why I ask myself how far Graham's sympathies went. Graham came close to thinking that it was Philby who had made the wisest choice.

Soizic: However, if what Norman Sherry reports is correct, Graham broke the rule of total loyalty towards Philby: he passed Philby's letters on to the Foreign Office.

Yvonne: No, not all of them. He only gave them the ones he thought would be of interest to them. In any case, he gave them the one about Afghanistan.* He told me that. When he left for England soon afterwards, and we had been discussing Kim's letter and his answer, he casually told me, 'I'm taking with me Kim's letter, together with my answer, because it may be information, it may be disinformation, so it's as well I take it to the Foreign Office.'

Soizic: And that's why he went to London?

Yvonne: No, he went because the occasion arose. There was nothing urgent about it.

Soizic: That's interesting . . . So what's your conclusion?

Yvonne: Graham has left us, taking his secrets with him. But what I can tell you is that, to the very end, he worked with the British Services.

---

* Letter dated 2 January, marked by Graham: '?80'; photocopy kept by Yvonne. Graham, in his last letter to me, also refers to the same letter from Philby: 'He [Philby] also wrote to me on the subject of the Afghan war saying that he was against it and that he knew nobody there who was for it – in other words, he indicated that the KGB had been against the war.'

14

A Sense of Friendship

Friendship, or a sense of friendship (rather as we say 'a sense of honour'), seems to have been one of the mainsprings of Graham Greene's personality. He experienced friendship in his life, just as much as he experienced love. But, first and foremost, he gave of himself.

And it would appear that he never expected any return, literally or otherwise, for as chance would have it his friends were very often taken far away, with or without return tickets, on dangerous journeys into the 'deadly zones of politics', as he sometimes called them. Or quite simply friendships were born, the outcome of those famous trips to more or less distant parts. It was in Cameroon that he met Yvonne, after all, and this through friends who were indirectly linked to his visits to Vietnam.

It also seems that Graham, a man who struck some people as being surly ('Trapped in loneliness', according to John Updike), was not as anti-social as has been made out. Even if an aura of solitude seemed to hover about him in his Antibes apartment, the reality was different, and he was never lonely. Yvonne said, 'Apart from his writing, he did not live a solitary life in the least. He did not feel lonely. In actual fact, he had a terrible time trying to preserve his solitude.' And yet he frequently and quite willingly emerged from his ivory tower. The letters Yvonne gave me to read provide proof of this. They recall soirées, conversations and personalities: Trevor Wilson in Vietnam, Bernard Diederich in Haiti and Santo Domingo, the priest Leopoldo Durán on the road and in monasteries in Spain. Yvonne was not always with him, owing to the ordering of their private lives, but she was present far more often than their common discretion would lead one to suppose, especially towards the end of his life. In this chapter, Yvonne speaks quite freely and in a way she had never done before (it was just before her own death) of all their lovers' jaunts, when they were particularly interested in *la douce France*.

In the little *Carnet rouge* Graham also jotted down remarks about places they had come across, and the people they had met. Throughout his life, however, he never confided his heart-aches to anyone except Yvonne and his sister Elisabeth. His interest in people was boundless, varied and enduring.

He needed other people, but not purely on an emotional level. As a writer, he made use of 'living' material. Yvonne mentioned, among others, Colonel Leroy, in Vietnam, and frequently Father Durán, of whom she said, 'He was more than a friend. For Graham, Leopoldo was a model for the novel he had in mind. It was a self-motivated friendship. The novel *Monsignor Quixote* is owed to him.'* Similarly, but in a much more anodyne way, in one of his short stories one comes across a comment I made to him in 1979, during a working lunch. Although our relationship was not particularly intimate, I had gone so far as to confess to him that I did not care for men with small ears. Well, a few years later, when *The Other Man* was published in Britain, a journalist told me, 'There's a striking resemblance between you and a character in a recent story of Graham's.' Not having read the story in question, and being extremely sceptical, I forgot the remark. But one day, with Yvonne at Vevey, I came across the book containing this story. One of the two characters, a Frenchwoman, a journalist by

---

* Yvonne pointed out that the royalties for *Monsignor Quixote* were divided equally between the monastery at Osera and the Sandinistas in Nicaragua, to help them in their struggle against the Somozistas.

profession, is interviewing a politician in South America. (I had made two trips to the Dominican Republic and had thought of visiting Haiti on the tracks of *The Comedians*.) The woman is called Marie-Claire. And, to crown it all, she 'disliked small ears'!

Examples to the contrary exist: Graham notably never made use of his friend Chuchu (a nickname meaning 'kiss-kiss'), Omar Torrijos's bodyguard, despite the fact that he wanted to bring him to life on paper; neither, ultimately, did he tell the story of my father in a novel, even though he wrote in his Prologue and Dedication to *The Other Man*, 'I've thought of it [writing a book about him] many times.'

There may be an indication of Graham Greene's 'addiction' to friendship and his liking for company (apart from what one notices in the letters to Yvonne, posted from the four corners of the globe, in which he complains – active lover that he was – of loneliness and her absence), and that is to be found in his dreams. In them, he was hardly ever alone.

He was always with a male or female friend. In real life, however, Yvonne pointed out that 'When he went somewhere with the idea of eventually (because it didn't always happen) writing something, he went on his own, having often made his contacts beforehand, through connections, etc.'

In fact, if we consider those who were closest to him, we very soon see that Graham lived in a rather 'padded' world in this respect. His brothers were very close to him and participated in his literary life; his sister, Elisabeth, was possibly his closest woman friend (together with Victoria Ocampo, according to Yvonne), being also his long-time counsellor (and his invaluable assistant after the departure of Josephine Reid, the devoted secretary); his niece, Amanda, was always diligent and warm-hearted; Caroline, his daughter, who almost fortuitously lived very close to him, in Switzerland, in the final days of his old age, as well as Martine, Yvonne's daughter, also living at Châno, near Vevey. To the end of his life, Graham kept an affectionate letter from Martine in his wallet, next to a photograph of

Yvonne.* And there was Francis, his son, conscious of his intellectual inheritance and very supportive, especially in Yvonne's vigilant mind, of the present memoir, who was often mentioned as well; Graham Carleton Greene, his nephew, who 'together with Amanda, went to a lot of trouble at the time of the funeral', and from whom Yvonne remembered receiving a change-of-address card from Albany, bearing the name 'Graham Greene' – the 'Carleton' having disappeared – which was 'the devil of a shock, so soon after Graham's death'.

It's impossible to mention them all. They form a family extended by notions of friendship, the 'closest' of them being those 'of his own generation', added Yvonne. 'Graham was not a family man, not in the least,' she warned. And if, as she told me, Graham once confessed rather movingly that I was in some ways his daughter, I must admit that he was far more than a friend, and that in the 'moments of agony' occasioned by our interviews, and in the trust and support he gave me, he was a kind of friendly father figure in my own life.

Soizic: So Graham was a man of 'extreme friendships'. I'm also thinking of Omar Torrijos with his curious 'charisma of despair', whose fine photograph attracted the attention of every visitor to Graham's home at Vevey.

But many of his friends did not necessarily dwell on 'the dangerous edge of things'. On gentler slopes we find in your own 'period', Yvonne: Leopoldo Durán, his Sancho Panza, as well as Robert Laffont, Charlie Chaplin, Tob Frere, Max and Joan Reinhardt . . . The scene is rich and varied.

In your view, were Graham's friendships elective of selective?

---

* The letter was shown and read to me by Yvonne. It is undated, but must have been written in 1969, or shortly afterwards: 'Dear Graham, Mummy told me you were sad and worried and that you were anxious about the future, and that particularly upsets me because I'd like to be able to do something for you and I feel very helpless. I just hope that everything gets sorted out very quickly and above all that you will be happy again because I love you very much.' Martine was just over eighteen at the time. Yvonne could not remember the cause of the 'worries' mentioned. [M.-F.A.]

Yvonne: I would say they were mostly elective. Each friendship was entirely private and depended on the person. But what marked Graham out from other people was that the equivalent of 'love at first sight' existed for him in friendships: it was a gift which was close to love. What is more, when he was talking about one or other of his friends, he used to say, 'I love him.' With Graham, it was all part of the same thing. It was true of your father, for example. What little he knew of him pleased and attracted him. They had things in common. And if Graham was not constant in love, there can be no doubt at all that he was a loyal and faithful friend: some of his travelling companions were with him for the greater part of his life. By and large, they all remained his friends. He kept up a continual relationship with them, either through meetings or through correspondence: letters were sacred to him, and he devoted a great deal of time and interest to them.

[Yvonne got up and went to look for some papers in Graham's bookcase at Vevey, and she showed me some letters from Herbert Read to Graham.]

Here, these are from Herbert Read, one of his closest friends, who died in the late 1960s. It's interesting to follow the course of Graham's life at a period when I did not yet know him. It's rather interesting and strange for me because Read's son, Piers Paul, seemed to go along, I would say, with Michael Shelden at the time his biography appeared.* And yet Graham had invited his father to Capri after he had had cancer of the tongue . . . I'm wandering off the point, but you see, he would have done anything for a friend. He was generous and willing to help, he would go to a lot of effort, he would travel and step into the breach if necessary, he would advise and encourage.

Soizic: Yes, the extraordinary thing is that he seemed to want others to write. He even telephoned me frequently from Paris or

---

* See *The Tablet*, 16 September 1986 in *Yours etc* where Graham Greene criticises Piers Paul Read for 'living rather out of the real world'.

Antibes to prompt me in this direction. 'But you're a writer, Soizic,' he told me when I protested my inability.

Yvonne: Indeed, how many times did he make me tell him the story of my adolescent years at the *lycée* in Quimper, a novel in itself, in his opinion! He tried to find out what I was like, about my past and all the anecdotes told in school. He loved hearing about all that, and then one day he said, 'Why don't you write it all down?' When we visited Quimper, we went to rue Briseux of course, and I found myself standing again in front of this huge oak door. Well, I was obviously moved, and I went in to inspect the high walls. And that was when he exclaimed, 'Why don't you try to write about . . .?' I replied, 'You see that was "*la boîte*". French people at that time called it "*la boîte*".' 'That would make a splendid title, "*La Boîte*", he added. And then later, in Capri, he took out some large sheets of paper and said, 'There, take a pen, you've got the paper. Write a first draft, and when you've finished the first chapter, the rest will come.' I never did it.

He was kind-hearted, you see. Writing, for him, was therapy, and he used to say that it would be so for others. He even went so far as to hold up Vivien as an example, showing me a book she had written about doll's houses and doll's-house furniture. He gave me extracts to read and he said, 'It's good, isn't it?' I replied, 'Yes, very good, very interesting.' He went on, 'I think she writes better than I do.' It was all said with great sincerity.

I'm thinking of one other example, which is the case of Georges Rosanov. He was a very well-known doctor in Nice. A stomach specialist. When we went to see him he told all sorts of anecdotes about his professional life. He was a Russian exile, very much in de-mand, the doctor employed by the railways, and 'the doctor' to call. He would go out at any time of the day or night to the Negresco. He attended all the classy people who stayed there. And Graham, sounding very good-natured, said, 'Why don't you write about all that?' One fine day, Rosanov decided to switch off a little and he invited us to his home. 'I've followed your advice,' he informed

Graham, 'and I've written a book called *A Funny Kind of Job*.' How he clung to him! Every time he completed a chapter, he showed it to him. But his stories, which were really spicy when he told them, were simply jotted down on paper and juxtaposed without any linking text. 'But, Georges, you need a connecting theme,' Graham told him, 'a link somewhere.' He never understood what that meant. The result was that on paper the stories were nothing.

Soizic: You give us a sympathetic portrait of Graham as 'friend'. But both of us know that he could also be extremely hostile, and so fearsome that people did not dare attack him during his lifetime, isn't that so? You mentioned Piers Paul Read at the time of the publication of Michael Shelden's biography. Isn't that the reverse of a certain coin? And then there were the kickbacks, such as Shirley Hazzard's book, and Anthony Burgess's disenchanted reaction after Graham's death, for example.

Yvonne: It's impossible to get involved in all that, Soizic. Burgess I've never understood. A writer's jealousy? That's sad. But Graham had many enemies; many journalists felt dissatisfied because they wanted to know more about the man himself, and about private concerns, etc. And you're in a very good position to know how difficult it was to squeeze anything out of him to do with his private life . . . All of a sudden, feeling frustrated, they would invent anything that occurred to them. But I can tell you that what Graham appreciated more than anything during our life together was to have succeeded in managing his affairs at last without rocking the boat, without causing too much commotion. Furthermore, I never had the sense that I was living with a famous or exceptional man. Never. We walked about quietly in the streets of Antibes, we strolled around Capri . . .

Soizic: But isn't what you tell me too good to be true, really?

Yvonne: Well, from time to time passers-by would murmur, 'He's a great writer.' As far as I was concerned, he was great by virtue of who he was, not because he was a writer. And fortunately, the way he behaved meant that we could go around unnoticed. Even the Chaplins, with whom we spent a lot of time, often observed this.

Soizic: You knew Charlie Chaplin on the Côte d'Azur?

Yvonne: Yes, through the Reinhardts. Graham thought highly of Charlie, particularly because Charlie, who was born in the gutter, went back, despite his success, to south London every time he visited England, so that he could rediscover the atmosphere of his childhood. Unlike others whom Graham mentioned, he did not look down on the poor. Anyway . . .

I remember a particular evening spent with Charlie when, all of a sudden, talking about his professional life, his films, et cetera, he started miming. Honestly, I felt as if I was watching a Chaplin movie. And yet he wasn't young. He must have been in his eighties at the time. He was such a clown! He would suddenly hide and then reappear like a jack-in-the-box, you know, with his smile and his white teeth, and those extraordinary blue eyes he had. Or there was the time on the boat: Joan Reinhardt had prepared some lobsters for lunch. I can still see him with his mass of white hair, very tanned, wearing his white bathrobe, and sitting beside the rails. He took a portion of lobster, part of the shell or some other bit, he ate it and then, oops, he tossed everything into the sea, whereupon Graham said, 'But Charlie, you're polluting the sea.' 'No, no,' he joked, 'it came from the sea and it's going back to the sea. The little fish will eat it and they'll be very pleased.' And then there was that occasion I briefly mentioned before, when we had lunched in the port at Villefranche – that's when that photograph I showed you was taken [June 1966]. There were the Chaplins, the Reinhardts, Graham and me. Charlie was sitting on one side of the table, Oona on the other. They were opposite one another. And very soon, naturally, the press arrived. They came very quickly. The bush telegraph had worked as it does in the African jungle . . . There was a group of three or four of them. They came up to the table. Charlie sat there, eating and talking, and he was quite happy. He was a hearty eater, you see. Oona, however, who had her back to the reporters – obviously, since those facing Charlie were standing behind Oona – said to him from time to time, 'Charlie, smile.' So he stopped eating, put down his napkin and looked up with a smile. Snap! The photo was taken, and Charlie continued eating as if nothing had happened. Afterwards, when we were leaving the table, he walked with rather jerky movements. Rather like the silent movies. Meanwhile, Graham had faded into the background.

All this is to show you that Graham made it his business not to attract the attention of the curious. Observing others is what a writer does.

Yvonne: Nevertheless, Graham was very impatient, even with some of his friends, and it brought him a certain amount of hostility. He didn't like people overstaying their welcome or engaging him on subjects which didn't interest him. I would see him growing restless and pacing around. You mentioned Shirley Hazzard's book, which was sometimes so harsh about Graham. I made some notes setting the record straight.* However, she wrote me a wonderful letter at the time of Graham's death, accompanied by a little note from Francis.† But her book shows that she did not really understand Graham. In fact, he rather kept out of her way sometimes, in Capri. He did not care for her brand of purely literary snobbery. That's why one day, to

---

* Not disposing of Yvonne's archives, I don't have a copy of this.
† Francis Steegmuller, Shirley Hazzard's husband, and the biographer of Flaubert. The note reads: 'I was a child when, through books and things, I first heard his "voice". A voice that spoke for many of us in the twentieth century. And that was true also of the artistic premise that, as Flaubert said, no writer of intelligence offers answers. Instead, they raise questions. No modern writer raised more pertinent questions than Graham, and one sees in so much that has been written about him since his death, how acutely these questions have troubled and stimulated his readers for a lifetime.'

avoid a prolonged evening and intellectual discussions, Graham said that we had to catch the last bus home. Shirley concluded from this that he was miserly and that he should have taken a taxi. You see how mistakes come to be made. Shirley, moreover, is a woman who writes very, very well.

Graham had a horror of snobbery, of intellectual snobbery and hypocrisy. Occasionally he got angry, especially when his friends were discussing literature. The strange thing is that this only ever happened among his friends. I noticed it very quickly at the beginning, when I began to make their acquaintance. So, there was a scene, for example, between him and Pat Frere: she started speaking about a book she had just read, and said she thought the book was wonderful and that the author was a great writer, etc. Graham happened to have read it: 'Oh, Pat, how can you say that? His book is awful.' She stopped, and then in no time at all she made a 180-degree turn, and this brilliant book and its brilliant author were no longer so wonderful. Well, he couldn't bear that. He said, 'But, Pat, you started saying this. Why, suddenly, do you turn like that?' That made him hopping mad.

He was impressive and all his friends were frightened of annoying him, whereas he was actually shy (it's a cliché to say so) and basically modest, and he was not big-headed, as they say, about his success. The day I told him that his friends were frightened of him in this respect, he was appalled. 'But it's awful what you're telling me!' he kept on saying.

Soizic: And yet, according to what you've told me, and to judge from his letters, on a social level and where human relationships were concerned, things became much easier. There were invitations to so-and-so's house, and to premières, and further invitations here and there. Graham had to be torn away, didn't he? Was it just because he was Graham Greene, perhaps?

Yvonne: No, I wouldn't say that, though there's probably some truth in it – it's a result of practice. However, he made a clear distinction between those who invited him privately (I'm no longer talking about official invitations, of course) just because he was Graham Greene, and his friends – those who, quite simply, were fond of him. It's true, too, that the fact that he was a well-known writer affected people's behaviour towards him.

Soizic: And even that of his friends, I'm sure.

Yvonne: Yes. In the beginning, when I met his friends – English friends, mostly – I noticed that people were a little suspicious of him; there was a certain reserve, I would even say apprehension.

Soizic: Didn't this help to put a sort of glass barrier between his friends and him, even the real ones?

Yvonne: No, no. He really did make a distinction. It irritated him terribly that there should be anything in his friends' behaviour which suggested that the reason they liked him so much was because he was Graham Greene. He hated toadying.*

Soizic: You were talking about his becoming 'hopping mad' just now, and said it only happened when it was to do with literature. Did he get 'hopping mad' like that with you, Yvonne?

Yvonne: Nearly. It was a close thing, sometimes. Between ourselves, there was one book that became almost a joke. It was *Sparkenbrook* by Charles Morgan. I had read it when I was very young, and had adored it. He said, 'I don't understand why.' (He didn't like Charles Morgan, you know.) He went on,

---

* Yvonne showed me a letter in which Graham was taking stock of his best friends and expressing praise or reservations according to their trustworthiness. I remember that my parents were mentioned, among others, my mother emerging with a few bruises, but I've forgotten the wording in the letter. As to Pat Frere, according to Yvonne, Graham told her, 'Be careful of Pat Frere.'

'It's full of clichés.' It's true that I had read the book when I was a girl. I haven't read it since. It's a book you remember, once you've read it. And Graham went on about it, because he almost despised you if you liked something he disliked. With him, it was never 'Tell me who your friends are and I will tell you who you are', but rather 'Tell me what you read and I will tell you who you are.' Well, with *Sparkenbrook*, I held my own. I told him, 'Look, I'm sorry. If I re-read it today, I might not have the same feelings about it, but I don't want to re-read it, I want to stay with my memories of it.' And that always bothered him over the years . . . After a certain period it was all forgotten, but I didn't give in. I'm sorry, but I liked that book!

Soizic: Breton women are stubborn!

Yvonne: Yes, you're right. And then, eventually, he found a different slant: 'Did you read it in the original version or in translation?' I replied, 'In translation,' for at the time I was totally incapable of reading in English. 'Well, that's it,' he rejoined, 'there must have been an excellent translator, and the clichés were cut out.' So that was the end of it. It was typical of him: he never let go. He wanted to take things to the bitter end.

Soizic: Would you say he was obsessive?

Yvonne: No, I wouldn't go as far as that. It was something that cropped up only at intervals, whereas obsession never leaves you. But he always put matters right, particularly where friend-ship was concerned. With the story of your father, for example, he never let go for as long as the enigma needed clearing up – and in his case, of course, one could always wait. Mind you, in that particular case it was not just a simple 'enigma' but the actual fate of a friend, who had inspired in him a feeling of rebellion as well as sadness, and right up to the end that bothered him.

Soizic: What were the other things – perhaps those in less tragic fields – that rankled with him or upset him during your life together?

Yvonne: Let me think . . . The fact that John le Carré said he was a 1930s writer. That did wound him. He was suddenly terribly hurt, and it remained with him. Each time he had an opportunity to talk to other people and ask their opinion, he used to bring up John le Carré's remark.

Soizic: So he harped on about things a lot?

Yvonne: Yes, he was stubborn and dogged.

Soizic: Vulnerable, too?

Yvonne: As well. Extremely fragile and vulnerable. He had great inner strength, but also great weakness, probably stemming from the humiliations he had experienced as a child. He was hypersensitive, always on the alert, and jibes wounded him and went straight to his heart. His enemies knew just how to handle him. Those who wished to harm him could do so easily through his work and his books. It bothered him, he went on and on talking about it, and I could feel how hurt he was. Of course, when he judged his enemies were justified, he took it very well. But not when he reckoned they were unfair. Spiteful words also affected him deeply, and even though he concealed it well, in private the bruises came out.

Soizic: Even if the hurt wasn't intentional?

Yvonne: No, of course not, but at moments like that he would say, 'Take it as it comes,' as they say. Though I think it's fairly unusual to harm someone without intending to do so. Somewhere, there's always the intention to hurt.

Soizic: So the reason he avoided literary critics and journalists, book fairs, conferences, seminars and other cultural or academic events may have been in order to protect himself?

Yvonne: No, I wouldn't go as far as that. Besides, he wasn't frightened of anything, you know, and furthermore he could be unpleasant to people he didn't like! No, all those things bored him enormously (he was always impatient). Actually, he hated high-flown theories about literature, he called it 'showing off'. I was certainly conscious of living with someone whose intellectual qualities were out of the ordinary, but Graham was not really an 'intellectual'. You know he refused to consider himself one. And that suited me. And yet we discussed everything – current affairs, politics, the latest news – very simply. But even the conversations he had with you exhausted him. He told me it was because 'I felt as if I was taking part in a play. But the worst thing was, the leading actor was me!' He felt as if he were playing a part.

Soizic: Yes, he wasn't an easy character.

Yvonne: When he was sad, for example, he had a tendency to get into bad moods. Or else he always saw two sides of the coin, the good and the bad simultaneously. Before he moved into his home in Antibes, for instance, he used to stay at the Hotel Royal, where he would spend a few days. Naturally, he was sad to have to go away and leave me. But every time he had to have an argument with the receptionist: they didn't come to collect his luggage quickly enough, or the bill hadn't arrived . . . He had to moan about something. To begin with, that shocked me. Yet he remained on very good terms with this receptionist for a long time afterwards. They used to chat when they ran into each other in town. So he was shy and uncommunicative generally, and he gave an impression of coldness. But when he felt he could trust someone, he was, on the contrary, very forthcoming, and not just with me, but with his friends. He was very open.

Soizic: All the same, it's not quite the impression I had.

Yvonne: In your case the circumstances were rather special. He was in the hot seat, but had agreed to play the game, out of friendship, so . . .

Soizic: Pressing him, as I was obliged to do, I was always frightened of unleashing furious bouts of anger or some sort of protest – which never happened. But I felt him capable of these kinds of reaction – for he *was* capable of them, wasn't he?

Yvonne: One has to admit that he could fly into a rage. Never with me, but I've observed such outbursts. One day, for example, we were at Fouquet's bar. I was talking to one of his friends, the husband of Marie Biche, his literary agent in Paris. Suddenly, I heard what sounded like an explosion. A very loud noise. I turned round. It was Graham, who had grabbed hold of an enormous china or pottery ashtray and had hurled it against the counter. Why? Because Marie Biche had started being critical of Alexander Frere. Graham would not tolerate people being criticised on the basis of hearsay. Anyway, Jean Biche paid for the drinks and we left Fouquet's, in single file, with Graham muttering something. The four of us took a taxi. We were deposited outside Graham's flat at 130 boulevard Malesherbes. When he got home, Graham was dreadfully pale and he looked terrible. All of a sudden he said, 'I'm sorry, but I feel sick. She started criticising Frere. She has never met him, and suddenly started taking what she had heard from here and there, which is absolute nonsense. I just couldn't bear her saying the very opposite of what Frere was.'

That anger, that flash of temper, just because a friend was being attacked, is also revealing of the reactions he could have. This was in 1961.

Soizic: But Alexander Stuart Frere was not just anyone. He was one of his closest friends, if not the best, wasn't he? And, as you've told me, his only confidant.

Yvonne: He had an enormous number of friends throughout the world. I would need pages to mention them and I would forget some of them. But there can be no doubt that in Graham's mind friendship had a name: that of Tob Frere. I need no better proof than the letter Graham sent me from the Royal Albion Hotel at Brighton on 7 September 1964: 'Today, I went to a fortune-teller on the pier . . . She cheered me a little by saying that I was going somewhere hot, by the sea, for a reunion. I had one great friend (male) whom I could rely on . . . Frere?'

The unwavering friendship between the two men went back a long way, to a crucial period in Graham's professional life, because Frere was already working, under Charles Evans's management, for the publishing house of Heinemann, who had published his first book, *The Man Within*, in 1929.*

Soizic: You used the the word 'unwavering'. Yet Graham could be fairly irascible – as we have seen with Marie Biche, who was nevertheless a great friend. Was Frere shielded from such eruptions?

Yvonne: Yes, more or less. I saw them quarrel only once, over Eric Ambler, who was also published by Heinemann. It was about a book of Ambler's on which their opinions differed. But, by and large, he had almost blind trust in Tob, based on a deep and most sincere friendship, which had elements of childishness in it: the story I recounted of the teddy-bear given to him by Frere, which Graham took with him on his travels, and which he mentioned in his letters to me, aroused misunderstandings and some unhealthy suppositions!

* Heinemann published all Graham's books up until 1961, including *A Burnt-Out Case*.

But let's talk about more serious things instead. I told you previously that the fate of *The Human Factor* lay in Frere's hands. Graham was not happy with the book, and he told me one day, 'I'm sending the manuscript to Frere, asking him to give me his opinion. If Frere decides it's not worth publishing, it will stay in a drawer; otherwise, I'll follow his advice.' And Frere's response on the telephone was: 'It's one of your best books; so you must publish it.' That shows the esteem he had for Frere.

To illustrate the friendship from another viewpoint, he even got angry with Malcolm Muggeridge in order to protect Frere. Muggeridge had let Graham know that he would like to be published by Heinemann. This was in the early sixties, when he was at work on *The Comedians* and before he left Heinemann. Malcolm was in a financial hole, and rather mixed-up, so Graham spoke to Charles Evans on his behalf (I think he was still running the firm at the time). He succeeded in getting him taken on by the publishing house, thanks partly to Frere, who had done his utmost to arrange it. And then, suddenly, Malcolm changed his mind and dropped everything, and Frere, who was in a senior position at Heinemann but was not yet in overall charge, was made to look foolish. And that was something Graham would not stand for.

Over the years, Frere climbed up the ladder, thanks to his professional qualities: he became a director, then chairman, and lastly president of Heinemann. Apart from their shared passion for books, the two men were bound by strong ties.

In the end, during the 1960s, when the publishing house was shaken by upheavals caused by financial problems, Frere felt he had been treated badly and even humiliated. So he decided, with much bitterness and resentment, to retire. He was then about sixty-four.

When Graham heard about what had happened, he took immediate action, left Heinemann and found a new home for himself at The Bodley Head, which at that time was run by Max

Reinhardt. Some other top authors, such as Georgette Heyer and Eric Ambler, followed his example.*

It was certainly a tough blow to Heinemann, and for Graham it was a wrench, but friendship had to supersede all other considerations.

In love, as in friendship, adversity often brings positive elements with it, and the epilogue to this relationship provides proof of this. Not only were Graham's feelings for Frere strengthened, but the behaviour of Max Reinhardt in the discussions and the generosity he showed touched Graham deeply. A new friendship was born; it continued until Graham's death. In fact, it was when he was at Providence Hospital, in Vevey, that Graham asked me to put together the material for the publication of the book about his dreams, *A World of My Own*. He added, 'And ask Max to publish it.' He had absolute trust in Max, just as he had had in Frere.†

Soizic: Would you say that Graham's friends came mainly from the world of publishing?

Yvonne: Yes, as I've already said. He obviously had many affinities with them, whatever their nationalities, and I should not fail to mention his friendship with Robert Laffont over a period of fifty years. Robert remained his publisher in France until his death.

* See the fine prefatory note to *The Comedians*, addressed to Frere: 'This is the first novel I have written since then [Graham's leaving Heinemann in 1961], and I want to offer it to you in memory of more than thirty years of association – a cold word to represent all the advice (which you never expected me to take), all the encouragement (which you never realized I needed), all the affection and fun of the years we shared.'
† It was because of this friendship that Yvonne, after Graham's death, agreed, on her own conditions, to see first Selina Hastings and afterwards Michael Shelden, who had both been recommended to her by Pat Frere. We know the consequences . . .

Soizic: What was his relationship, generally speaking, with other writers, male or female?

Yvonne: In England his best friends among writers were undoubtedly Evelyn Waugh and Herbert Read. The eccentricity of the former fascinated him; and the discretion and humility of the latter attracted him. As I told you, he often spoke to me about them. In Capri, Peter Glenville and Bill Smith came to our house. He used to see Kenneth McPherson, Islay Lyons, and the group of people around Norman Douglas, whom he literally adored. They were principally intellectuals, writers and artists. He admired them for their intrinsic qualities. It did not bother him if they were homosexuals – given that, despite the gossip, Graham obviously had no leanings of that sort. (When he was asked the question, he replied, 'No, I've never had any homosexual experiences, but I take no credit for it, for I've never been tempted. The experience of life in a community, among young boys of my own age in dormitories when I was a boarder at Berkhamsted, cured me of that for good.')

As to the period covering our life together, he numbered a good many writers among his friends. I'm thinking particularly of Gloria Emerson, Gabriel García Márquez, Mario Soldati, Paul Theroux (though with him things also turned a little sour eventually).* Writers and young people very often sent him their books and Graham, as you know, would say openly whether he liked something or not. So his views were not always well taken . . .†

Soizic: Your life seems to have been devoted to Graham, but it's also been a fascinating life – all those remarkable men and women you met . . .

* No trace of any disagreement in the case of Theroux, whom I interviewed in 1992; on the contrary, only an immense and affectionate admiration for Greene.
† Among people he helped or supported, Yvonne mentioned Muriel Spark, R. K. Narayan, Vladimir Nabokov, Charlie Chaplin.

Yvonne: Oh yes! All I've seen, too. Those telephone calls from all four corners of the globe, I found very interesting. And having to spur him on. 'Come on! Come on!' Because, when he had writer's block, it affected his mood quite apart from his writing. I was thrilled by the events, and stimulated by the people I met through him. I was almost shattered by the fate of Pablo Neruda, the sage, whom we had seen in Paris. It was towards the end of his life and he was already very ill. This exiled man, who could no longer do anything for his country, who had this extraordinary gift as a poet, and yet who accepted, with much bitterness, the blows of fate . . . Someone else who impressed me greatly was Moshe Dayan, in Israel. Graham had already met him there.

Soizic: Did you become friends with him?

Yvonne: No, I wouldn't say friends. To begin with, he was already in very poor shape physically. This was shortly before his death in 1981. We had lunch with him and his wife. You see – and I bring this up for consideration when people talk about Graham's anti-Semitism . . . But what really brought about Graham's great admiration for Israel was the Entebbe operation, and the way they went about overthrowing Idi Amin.*

And then there were also particular instances, or exceptional circumstances, such as the meeting with the astronaut Grechko, who had taken *Our Man in Havana* with him into space, and who, when Graham travelled to the Soviet Union in 1987, presented him with the copy (now in a library in the United States). Graham was moved to tears. Grechko had learnt English thanks to this book, which he had read fifty times!

Soizic: How social was Graham's literary life after he moved to France?

* They did not, of course. But in July 1976 Israeli forces did carry out a successful commando raid on Entebbe airport, Uganda, to free the hostages in a hijacked aeroplane.

Yvonne: Well, he stopped frequenting literary circles altogether. He found the celebration of François Mauriac's eightieth birthday on 11 October 1965, at the Ritz in Paris, so painful that he decided to give up those kinds of festivities for good.

Soizic: Why was that?

Yvonne: It was too great a test for his shyness when Mauriac, in his speech of welcome, specially thanked his friend Graham Greene for having crossed the Channel to celebrate his birthday. He continued to maintain relationships, albeit only occasional, with Mauriac, Maurice Druon, Max Gallo, Alain Peyrefitte, Michel Déon, Paul Guimard and Michel Droit, for example.

Soizic: You mention very few women among these literary friendships . . .

Yvonne: Just a moment . . . You mustn't think that his friends were almost solely men. I've even prepared a little list, such as it is, of Graham's women friends:* Elizabeth Bowen; Edith Sitwell [crossed out and reinserted in fourth position]; Muriel Spark; Victoria Ocampo (Argentina); Jeanne Stonor; Marie Biche – then Michelle Lapautre; and, above all, his sister Elisabeth; Laetitia Cerio on Capri and the Dottoressa Moor; Valentina Ivacheva; Tania Lanina; Tatiana Koudriavsheva; Gloria Emerson;† Maria Newall (who lived in Portugal, and for a long time in Albania) – a friend of Leopoldo Durán's.

* This handwritten list is all the more precious since Yvonne, at the end of her life, which came so abruptly, could hardly write any more. I have had to add in my own hand three names, which she dictated to me, as well as her account of her travels around France with Graham. This was without the security of a tape-recorder, which she didn't want me to use at this stage.
† Whose book, *Loving Graham Greene* (New York: Random House, 2000), has been published since these conversations took place.

Soizic: It's clear that Graham didn't like bluestockings. Nor did he much care for the 'hens', as he called them, 'those hundred per cent feminine women with a Harrods accent', you once explained to me. You added, 'And even a certain masculinity did not displease him, as with Victoria Ocampo.' But wasn't he only really at ease among his male friends?

Yvonne: No, I don't think so. I told you that each friendship was special in its own way. It depended on individuals. They couldn't be divided according to sex, or even sexuality. Graham couldn't care less about that. What mattered was sincerity, and the genuineness of people in relation to their lives. If your mother, for example, had done what your father had done with his life, it would have been she who became his friend. He would have done for her what he did for him. He might even have admired her the more, being a woman doing such things.

Furthermore, I heard him give his opinion about women when Margaret Thatcher was elected for the first time . . . And yet she was a member of the Conservative Party. Graham looked very happy when he heard the results – 1979, wasn't it? To my astonishment, he explained, 'It doesn't make a great difference with us, Labour or Conservative, in day-to-day life, or even in politics. But I'm pleased mainly because, for once, it's a woman.' 'What do you mean by that?' He replied, 'Because I find that women, in general, are more intelligent, more honest and more courageous than men.' So when people say he was a misogynist, they're completely wrong. For example, he couldn't bear me to spend five minutes in the kitchen. No, he wasn't the sort who makes women work.

He liked and valued women. You knew him; did you ever come across the slightest reservation or condescension on his part, or the slightest attitude of, let us call it, 'machismo'?

Soizic: At the time, it didn't occur to me. It seemed to me that he saw me as a person. On that score, he probably made sure that I felt, despite my terrible feeling of awe, that I was almost on an equal footing with him. Like a friend, after all.

Soizic: You told me he liked women with a masculine side to them. Do you think that you have any of those masculine elements?

Yvonne: Yes, I think so. At any rate, I wear trousers a lot! Yes, I don't think I'm a hundred per cent feminine.

Soizic: Apart from that, could you say a little more about it?

Yvonne: Well, it's not just the way one dresses. He also considered that women needed to have the right blend of hormones, by which he meant that they should not depend entirely on men, that they should take control of themselves, and, he would add humorously – he, who never learnt to drive – that 'they should know how to drive a car'!

Soizic: Can you think of examples of other women, who were not necessarily his mistresses, but who had a touch of masculinity that pleased him?

Yvonne: I would say that apart from Vivien, who was truly feminine, all the women who mattered to him in his life had this slightly masculine side. He often told me, for example, that Dorothy (poor woman, she became very fat), whom he met during the Blitz, had attracted him because of her slightly urchin looks, with her cap and her brave, boyish manner, and her many normally male qualities.

Soizic: Isn't that why, in spite of the fact that a number of Graham's friends were homosexual, certain biographers have extrapolated and imagined all sots of penchants – aside from his talent for spotting and describing homosexuality? I'm thinking of *May We Borrow Your Husband?*, for instance? I'm reminded, too, of what you told me, and what we know about the Catherine Walston period: she used to accompany Graham to brothels, disguised as a boy or a man. Perhaps she struck a perverse chord in Graham – the one who did his evil deeds for him – in some way, didn't she?

Yvonne: Perhaps. He would never have admitted it. He never accused Catherine of anything. He only ever spoke well of the women he had had affairs with.

Soizic: You're not telling me everything. Didn't you, too, strike this perverse chord?

Yvonne: No, in actual fact, I never found anything perverse, in that sense of the word, about him . . . Apparently, I once told your mother that Graham and I had the same vices. But the only vice was that we shared the same temperament. When we walked through the piazza on Capri, he would notice beautiful women and tell me so, but it was very innocent. Besides, I was always amazed and wondered why he crossed the harbour to take the ferry to Naples and go to the brothels with Catherine. Now, who was leading whom? That's the problem.

Soizic: The problem, if there is one, is not knowing who was leading the other – there was clearly some kind of osmosis. But they must have caused pain to one another – pain to those around them, no?

Yvonne: When you read the second volume of Norman Sherry's biography, you realise that there were two kinds of monster confronting each other. And Graham spoke to me of the scenes of jealousy between them. They were appalling.

Soizic: They probably enjoyed all that, at the time.

Yvonne: Yes, probably. Graham liked it, Catherine liked it. For, as you say, there's generally osmosis. But what motivated her? That's what I ask myself. Why . . .?

Soizic: You ask in relation to her, not to him. That's surprising, isn't it?

Yvonne: Because I think that he . . . Well, he was able to adapt perfectly to the woman he was living with.

Soizic: So he must have been rather weak, then – with women?

Yvonne: No. No. The wish to please and bring happiness, and to give pleasure. That would be what motivated him, in my view, both in that respect and in many others, particularly friendship.

Soizic: But you don't do all that, whatever the conditions, in order to 'give pleasure'.

Yvonne: No. There are limits, all the same. And, as it happened, they did no harm to anyone but themselves.

Soizic: Would you say that Graham was a masochist, at that time? After all, he knew Catherine had other lovers.

Yvonne: I even think that it was she who told him . . . No. He was hysterical. To share her with the husband because things weren't going well between her and Harry, if need be, yes, but to share her with another lover, surely not. So I would say that she managed to gain forgiveness, and he, too, on his side, would look around elsewhere.

Soizic: Do you tell yourself that you had a narrow escape, having met him just after this period?

Yvonne: Not at all. That type of question never cropped up between us. There was none of that perverse aspect, that sort of mania for crushing oneself.

Soizic: So it wasn't something that was vital for him?

Yvonne: No, no. We have the proof. Everything worked out very well without all that. And I would even say that in his heart of hearts he felt a sort of comfort in not having all those side issues any more.

Soizic: But how can you know?

Yvonne: Because, when he spoke to me about that period, he was amazed. That he could have put up with it, that he could have done all that. He was amazed.

Soizic: In what way?

Yvonne: That it was completely preposterous.

Soizic: How would he put it in English, for example?

Yvonne: 'I was completely, completely out of my head', or 'I just don't understand what happened during those . . .' He spoke about it, you might say, like a man emerging from a nightmare.

Soizic: So, despite what you told me earlier, for Graham there was a great difference between love and friendship, for his friendships appear to have been less stormy, and they endured for life.

Yvonne: Graham was passionate as a human being, just as he was as a lover. But as to friendship, yes, with just a few exceptions, it was for life, and even the after-life! For the majority of his friends have remained my friends since his death . . . I'm thinking of

Gloria Emerson, again, of Alberto Huerta. I've corresponded with a number of them, and some have been to see me, at Vevey or Juan-les-Pins. Carole (Caroline) invited me to her home and visited me at Châno, Amanda has been a darling, as have Louise and Nick Dennys, his nieces and nephews; that's on the family side. In Paris, Michelle and René Lapautre have always been available. I haven't felt neglected. Tanya Lanina, Graham's interpreter in the Soviet Union, Tatiyana Kudriyavsteva and Rufa Philby made the journey to Juan from Moscow. My great friend Ruth Lazarus and I even went to stay in Miami with Bernard Diederich and his wife, in 1998 – remember it was Bernard who introduced Graham to Torrijos . . . The friendship is still there. They loved Graham, whether they had met him in person or not. I think of the Trappist monk Ralph Rite, and of Julian Evans, who came to see me in Vevey; Ralph came twice to Juan as well. I have corresponded with them. I've had many friendly phone calls and friends continue to write to me, like the Vizinczeys, Gloria and Stephen. You see, I have not been abandoned!

Soizic: Do you remember, a few years ago, when we started working on this book, you gave me two little photographs of Graham, identity photos of him in his final years. On the back of one of them, you had written: 'I'm taking care of you', and on the other: 'I'm counting on you'? Here. Look . . .

Yvonne: It's strange, I'd forgotten. Yes, it's certainly my handwriting.*

Soizic: Doesn't that illustrate, almost as if deliberately, two aspects of his personality, one fairly obvious, the other more secretive?

---

* There is an interesting misunderstanding in this dialogue, owing to the fact that Yvonne and I had worked on this book over a long span of time. She had forgotten her intention when writing these words on the back of the photographs. In retrospect, 'I'm counting on you' probably meant 'I want you to finish that book.'

Yvonne: 'I'm taking care of you', of course, is really him. He had such vitality, such presence. When he died, you can imagine, the people around him; my daughter Martine, for example – oh, I don't want to bother her with that or with my own grief, but I know it was painful for her. She loved him very much. She, like me, but to a lesser degree, naturally, had that feeling of being an orphan . . .

Soizic: He protected people, certainly. But who was he protected by? If he was.

Yvonne: Now, I don't see it like that at all. I wonder in what way he needed protection? I don't know.

Soizic: Isn't that the least recognised aspect of him, which you are bringing to light with this 'I'm counting on you' that you make him say?

Yvonne: I don't think so. Yes, he needed company, but protection . . . The only person who could have protected him was Elisabeth, his sister, although she was nine years younger than him. I think the opposite occurred. He protected her, too. But when Elisabeth became seriously ill, one has to remember it was her daughter, Amanda, who took up the reins. It wasn't a simple secretarial job, for Elisabeth, don't forget, knew all about Graham's past, and besides, having worked in the Secret Service, her savoir-faire was incalculable. Amanda said at the time, 'Uncle Graham, don't worry, I'll do my best. I'll take over and do the job while my mother is . . .'

Soizic: And today? I wouldn't say that you protect him, but you watch over the manes. Everything revolves around Graham's life. Admiration? Adoration?

Yvonne: Both. If I take things to heart, it's because I have a feeling of injustice. My instinct would have been not to say anything to anyone. Our life together was his, it was mine. But, as you've seen yourself, I've gone a very long way, all the same.

Soizic: Do you think so? I haven't actually asked you very direct questions.

Yvonne: Perhaps not. Perhaps you may not have asked me direct questions, and I've been the one who wanted to tell everything . . .

Soizic: Everything . . .

Yvonne: Well, the truth. The need to re-establish the truth, the man, the writer.

15

Travels with Yvonne

'Graham adored crossing frontiers,' Yvonne told me. 'Why do I go to Nicaragua?' he once said to Philby. 'Because I have a consuming curiosity.'* But Graham also liked his routine, lunches at Chez Félix at Antibes, with Yvonne's dog Sandy. ('He never loved an animal as he loved Sandy,' she said.) 'He needed an everyday life,' she recalled. 'Yet he was at ease anywhere and he could have written on his knees. What's more, if he liked Capri and his little study at the Villa Rosaio, it was because he felt the need to be as if in a cage.' Then she observed, 'Brighton also had that effect on him. He needed that town in order to cut himself off.' Sometimes he travelled in a perilous and Spartan way, sometimes he was not averse to a certain comfort, even to a certain luxury, whereas, Yvonne asserted, 'he could not have lived in luxury or even in a bourgeois atmosphere'. On one occasion, he went away on his own, far away, without her. With an idea for a novel in mind, for example, 'vaguely about Panama and General Tor-rijos'. 'Chuchu,' she said, 'sent him his ticket every year at the same time, in the summer, while I was taken up with . . . He had no precise plan, and he did not speak about it in advance, not because he was a secretive man but for the very good reason that he never knew beforehand what he was going to do,' she

* Graham in a letter to Kim Philby, 30 July 1980.

explained. 'At another time, the two of us would escape to Barbados almost every year to join the Freres, or perhaps to Austria, to Washington, to Moscow, to almost all the countries of Europe, or it might be just to the Colombe d'Or, at Vence.' He travelled 'more out of necessity than from a desire to travel . . . But also from necessity', she added.

So what truth can be established from such paradoxical, versatile material? Sometimes, Yvonne herself didn't seem quite sure . . .

Soizic: Would you say that one of Graham's favourite utterances, 'My roots are in rootlessness', was still true when it came to his life with you?

Yvonne: I don't really know. It's only when I re-read the letters I received from him over the course of years that I realise he was rather unsettled by our forced separations, while I, for my part, was very busy with the children. For our summer holidays, with Jacques and my daughters, we used to go to Switzerland.* During that time, one has to say that he wandered around like a lost soul. Perhaps it's precisely this that created the legend of the lonely man. In one of the letters, for example, he wrote, 'I'm in London, I thought of going to Brighton, but I don't know – or else, to Paris.' You see, he hadn't much of a clue . . . In other letters at the beginning, he said, 'I'm terribly depressed', 'feel very lonely', 'I'm in a bad mood'. He often signed off, 'Your lonely lover'.

Soizic: And yet it was at that period, 1963 onwards, when he was preparing to write *The Comedians*, a project he was very involved in, when he was taking physical risks to denounce the horror of a political situation . . .

Yvonne: Yes. His involvement led him to Haiti, later to Cuba, and then throughout Central America, almost every year. There,

---

* Jacques is Swiss.

as far as his melancholia went, it was still all right, because things were new to him, he was out of his usual surroundings. But when he returned from his travels I was not always available, and that period of floundering would start up . . . That was why we decided to shorten our separations, which often lasted for two months, and to meet even if it were only for three or four days. Afterwards, he would set off again and things were better. But in his letters, indeed, you can glimpse that kind of languor. It used to surprise me. I was aware that he got bored, but later we were together again, and it was all forgotten, as it were.

Soizic: No doubt. But what surprises me is that for a man of his 'impetuous' temperament, not in the least 'dimmed' (to use his word) by age and, let us say, maturity, two months is a long time . . . however much you tell me that he often said in his letters, 'I was *sage*', 'I was totally *sage*', '*sage* – except in dreams'. And yet he seemed to take it all in good humour, witness this photograph which you had copied for me. We see him there in Cuba, tall, relaxed and a bit gauche, with his baggy trousers, surrounded by laughing friends, all much shorter than him. On the back there is this inscription, half in English, half in French, of which you have allowed me to reproduce only the first words: 'I was very *sage*. Nothing much there to hold my tights up.' Despite the humour, wasn't it difficult, all the same? You had the tougher role.

Yvonne: That's true. Especially as he had calmed down, or become more '*sage*', only in the sense that he had learnt his lessons from the past and was more prudent with women. Anyway, I think I was right to trust him. And, as I've already told you, I didn't regret my decision not to get a divorce in order to move in with him. I said no, because each time we were apart, afterwards it was like starting afresh. I'm not certain it would have lasted so long had we lived together the whole time. Especially with children to bring up.

Soizic: Nevertheless, he could have chosen not to travel so much and to stay quietly nearby, in Antibes.

Yvonne: Oh, you know, Antibes . . . Even in Paris, where we only went for holidays, he could no longer bear feeling lonely. It was the same surroundings, but nothing was the same any more.

Soizic: You mean without you?

Yvonne: Yes. He had a need to escape. In any case, he had always been a compulsive globetrotter. Travel for him was a necessity. Everything interested him.

Soizic: When did his first period of absence occur, as far as you were concerned?

Yvonne: Oh, he went away so often! Wait: the very first time, he went off for a week or so to Cap Ferrat, to La Voile d'Or, with the Reinhardts, then he went back to London. He would go back and spend a few days there, then leave again, because at that time he was still based in England.

Soizic: What did you know about his movements? Were you anxious about him?

Yvonne: He didn't talk to me beforehand about the circumstances of his journeys, even though he told me about them, of course.

Soizic: You didn't go with him. Well, not often – or did you?

Yvonne: Not to Latin America. He always said it was too dangerous for me. And yet . . . We had started to think about it . . . You see . . . The two regrets that he had – or three, I should say – were not to have been present at Aristide's investment in Haiti; yet, equally, he very much wanted to go back to Cuba, and then he would have taken me with him. In 1988 and 1989, worrying rumours reached him which reinforced his doubts about Fidel, and he wanted to see for himself – really – see what was going on. His third regret was not to have been able to meet Havel again, after the Velvet Revolution in Prague. It was clear that I was to accompany him. So I didn't feel as if I was kept at arm's length or left out, or 'uninvolved' with him. That only happened once during our life together, at the beginning of our relationship, when we went to London together, and there, in his flat, the Catherine Walston photograph episode. That very nearly did cause us to break up, as I explained before.

Was I anxious about him? No, not particularly. I'm not anxious by nature, and I only knew about things once he was back, as on the occasion when, just after the Six-Day War, he had to stay behind following an incursion into Golan. Only once was I anxious about him. It was when he went off on some sort of mission to Northern Ireland. He was quite worried himself, and he admitted it.

Soizic: Did he talk to you about his earlier journeys, or the people with whom he travelled?

Yvonne: Yes, of course. I remember, incidentally, a story he told me about his trip to Liberia with his cousin Barbara. (I met her once, at lunch, with his sister, Elisabeth.) How he made me laugh when he told it to me the first time! He kept up a very good relationship with her. There was a great deal of affection between them. He told me that at the end of their journey to Liberia they were so tired and so exhausted before he became ill – because he almost died there, from a terrible fever (Barbara actually wrote a book about the trip). Well, he was telling me, I don't know why, that Barbara was wearing thick socks, because they were walking in the bush, and that those socks kept slipping, and that it got on his nerves terribly. It was funny, this image of slippery socks and the way it made him laugh all those years later. And he never dared tell her, because he didn't want to annoy or upset her. But it got on his nerves. They never quarrelled, which is fairly astonishing in travelling conditions such as they were forced to endure. But that night when he was so ill . . . What was Barbara to do? Graham was half dead. In the state he was in, she thought, 'It's not possible, he'll never recover.' She had already lit a small candle to put beside him. A sort of death vigil. She imagined him dead. And she would have to return alone, through the bush! How awful! [*Laughter*]

Soizic: And what were the 'Travels with Yvonne' like?

Yvonne: Very happy. We travelled about a lot together, for periods of a fortnight. Everywhere, or almost.

Soizic: What was he like at those times? Nervous? Or, on the contrary, calmer than usual?

Yvonne: No, he wasn't nervous. However, there was always that worry about being on time, not missing his plane. Oh yes. We had to be at the airport one or two hours beforehand. He was actually quite prudent. Not especially because he was with me, I think. He had been a great traveller, as everyone knows; but he was full of contradictions, and in reality he enjoyed the same procedure each day. Everything was calculated: the ritual of our whisky time, for instance, or our gin time, or vodka time, depending on the latitude. (By the way, we're talking about him as if he was an inveterate drunkard. In thirty years, I never saw him drunk. Never. You see how legends take root. I could tell when he had drunk a little, from the way he talked. He took on the slight lisp he had when he was a child. But I never saw him drunk.) We had some marvellous trips, particularly in the late 1980s, to the Soviet Union, among other places, several times. For example, in 1986 we went to Moscow, Leningrad, Georgia, and then back to Moscow again.

Every year we also went on jaunts around France. It's through him that I came to know my own country. We would choose a region, the Jura, say. I discovered a fabulous country, full of trout rivers. One Sunday, in a little restaurant, the owner offered us some *vin jaune*. It was as if we were with an old friend. Paradise! We forgot the outside world and we lived just for ourselves. From the very beginning. Sometimes we went no further than the Colombe d'Or or the Auberge de Noves.

For me it was also a world I hadn't known existed. I was amazed by the Colombe d'Or: the peasant woman showing up, *Vovonne la bretonne* from the *occoté* [sic: other shore] of the sea! In the Grand Hotel in Rome, I must admit that I did feel a bit lost. I would never have imagined such a place existed. A new world. My whole life changed. Occasionally, I remember, I moved about like a robot to begin with. The day he took me to the Hotel de Paris, at Monte Carlo. The reception hall was immense. You could have entered on horseback! I was very ill at ease. Uprooted. I said to myself, 'I hope our life together won't be like this.' Afterwards, I got used to it. For him, it was just fantasy.

On official journeys, it wasn't the same. But on others, we very often hired a car. I drove. He was very good at finding nice inns to stay in. He would go through the *Guide Michelin* with a fine-tooth comb. That place we stayed at in the Camargue . . . my God! The first night, at Pont de . . . I've forgotten – where they breed the birds. We didn't close our eyes all night. It was like *À nous la liberté* [Freedom is Ours]. I got tired more easily than he did . . . One day, we were stopped by the Tour de France, near one of those little villages in Provence. At the restaurant, we drank two or three bottles of the house wine between us. It was incredibly precious. When you're happy, you appreciate being alone, and everything is marvellous. What's more, we went to some very beautiful places. Sandy, my dog, was with us most of the time, and he recognised the route to the Auberge de Noves. There was a donkey there. I said to Sandy, 'She's still there, the silly plump creature.' What filled me with joy was to see Graham relaxed. He forgot about everything. He brought nothing to write with. No paper. Nothing. There were no worries about the books he had in mind. He cut off completely. We were as one. It brought us close together. We returned with our love rejuvenated. We played around like children (when one thinks of this image of the serious, solemn Greene – which existed!). He knew how to become just like anyone else, leaving his cares behind him.

Those kinds of trips began under favourable auspices: three nights at the Colombe d'Or, for example. The owners told us, just as we were leaving, that for artists the first visit was free. We could have stayed for a week! Next, the Auberge de Noves, south of Avignon, near Châteaurenard. Set on its own, in the country-side. We stopped there to take an aperitif. Monsieur Lallemand, the owner (the *Guide Michelin* said 'handed down from father to son'), came to see us. Privileged treatment. He recommended the chef's specialities. Two plates with a sauce which was so good that we decided to spend the night there. But there were no bedrooms left, apart from one with a single bed. We slept in it. It was like an adventure, a luxurious one. He could afford that. And there were our trips to Brittany, staying at country hotels one night, and at inns with creaking beds the next.

But I also liked Capri. Twice a year. Working holidays. He took his work with him, but they were holidays all the same. Capri was best of all! It was one big party. I would never want to go back there without him. He once suggested that I get back his house (now owned by a Roman lawyer, who has preserved its exterior). Why Capri? Catherine and he had already fallen in love with the island. Norman Douglas and the Contessa Cerio – their friend, who was the 'soul' of Capri, and whose father had been mayor three times – were already there. And also the Dottoressa, with her two rabbit teeth. She was very funny. Shirley [Hazzard] never understood why Graham was interested in her. She used to tell such stories . . . She was a doctor and she looked after the poor for nothing. There was a very friendly atmosphere on Capri, and a great deal of love.

Soizic: Or luvvies?

Yvonne: Ah yes! Lots of lesbians and homosexuals [*laughter*]! Laetitia was in the know and told us everything. Even Graham told me (and he owed a lot to Agnello, the estate agent) that when he bought the villa it was lived in by a Swedish woman who had a young lover who was 'turning homosexual'. When they set off to see the notary, to buy the house, the fellow pinched Graham's bottom. The Swedish woman then went off with her young lover. They both had narrow escapes.

Soizic: You made a strange pair of gossips.

Yvonne: That was the kind of story Graham liked to hear. He did love gossip. With Laetitia, no one well known could escape her. According to Graham, 'there was magic in the air', and as far as possible he used to begin his books there. Work seemed easier. We went there in 1989, in the spring. His last novel, *The Captain and the Enemy*, was partly written there.

Graham's friends adopted me without any problem. Catherine Walston had lived on the fringe of things there, and she didn't speak a word of Italian. I managed fairly well on that score. Gemma, the owner of the restaurant where we always ate, did not speak a word of English, and Graham not a word of Italian, so I made a particular effort to learn the language. In the morning, Agnello, who had built Da Gemma, would come. Everyone liked him. Every evening, Carmela looked after the house, the domestic chores and the garden. At lunchtime, we used to go and eat at her house. Except for the day when Graham was made an honorary citizen. Laetitia was going to be the interpreter, and since she had come to us I had cooked an omelette. On that great day, the Archbishop of Sorrento had come over for the ceremony. You should have seen them, all those gentlemen in dark suits, who gathered beneath the Villa Rosaio, then moved on to the town hall, and then to the Church of San Michele. Carmela's son read three lines, and then burst into tears, he was so moved!

And you can't know how I felt when I sailed past Capri, on a cruise with my friend Ruth Lazarus, in 1999. Capri was so much associated with our life . . . a dream life.

16

The Black Clock

Throughout his life, Graham Greene enjoyed dicing with death; flirting with it; making fun of it. For many readers and for people who were close to him, he embodied that 'laughter in the shadow of the gallows' described by a Swedish critic.

If, during the last fifteen years of his life, he had not 'sought out death deliberately' as he put it, it was nevertheless the counterpoint to his lust for life, which fused with his desire to write, something which survived to the very end, just as mutual love had done.

But had this death-defying man changed? Had he, as it were, tamed the Grim Reaper? Once death's shadow fell, how would he cope? Had it altered his concept of 'an unforgiving wall', a bleak remark he made in 1979, and had there been any atonement in those doubts he expressed at the time? 'I'm just not bothered. I'll have it sorted out soon enough . . . or else I won't.'* What did he say? What did he do? What was the impact, in his final hours, of the presence of Yvonne, who had hoped, as she confided, to be 'the last one left standing on the platform' so that she could spare her beloved 'the punishment of absence'?

Amid the snowy slopes of Switzerland, in early April 1991, with his lover close to him, Graham made his final conversion. And it would seem that he succeeded in transforming the 'end' into a 'beginning', as if, in that cruel month of April, with

* *The Other Man*, p. 173.

Yvonne at his side, he had already started upon that famous 'for ever and the longest day'.

In August 2001, in the wake of those endless years, Yvonne, with all her memories and her unquenchable passion intact, but still quite ill when I believed her to be cured, was following in his tracks – just as a lover would do. Lying on one of the twin beds in the room we were sharing at Juan-les-Pins, surrounded by scattered documents which she had continued to consult eight or ten hours a day and late into the night, even though she could no longer use her hands to write, Yvonne, like a schoolgirl, had, with a furtive and surprising gesture, just kissed a photograph of Graham ('so handsome') on the cover of an old magazine.

And then, however odd it may seem, just as we were completing this chapter, she finally decided to turn her own last page.

These two people were reunited at last. I grieve for them both.

Soizic: During the very last period of his life, how did this man whom you had known for thirty-two years strike you?

Yvonne: What I find curious is that it should be the strongest aspects of his character that stood out: curiosity and the desire to know; that lucidity and preciseness. All this combined with something new: a great serenity.

At Providence Hospital, in Vevey, about a week before his death, when he knew he would not live, he said to me, 'After all, it may be an interesting experience; at last I shall know what lies on the other side of the fence.'

He said this calmly, very calmly. There was even a light in his eyes. He was interested. 'I shall know the answer to our questions.' He added, 'I wonder whether I shall see the intense bright flash that those who have been in a coma and come back to life talk about.'

A little earlier, in the flat at Châno – he had difficulty getting about, but he was still able to walk (a week before his death, he was even doing a hundred paces) – he had made another remark to me: 'If we human beings come on this earth only in order to spend about eighty years here, that makes no sense. What is eighty years compared to eternity? Nothing. So there must be something else.' You see how he was trying to convince himself that there is a life after death. In fact, he was already living in the next world.

Soizic: Would you say that from then on he had a different perception of the afterlife?

Yvonne: Yes, he had spent his whole life asking himself that question. But doubt remained, as you remember. And then suddenly, with that remark, he found the answer: there was an afterlife. Death was not an 'end' but a 'beginning'.

What's more, I believe it was discovering this that gave him this incredible serenity. There was actually never any panic. He really was ready to die. Once you have accepted death, you're no longer frightened of it.*

Soizic: Do you think that his illness, which had become apparent over the past two years, had also helped prepare him for death?

Yvonne: Probably. It's true, in fact, that one or two years earlier he had seemed to be suffering from bouts of great weariness, which they thought was mental exhaustion. He had gone to spend Christmas in Switzerland with his daughter Caroline, and one morning, very suddenly, he collapsed. He had to be taken to the hospital at Vevey. After a number of examinations and tests, they discovered that

---

* I should add that some weeks after I had completed this manuscript, I heard from Amanda Saunders, Graham's niece, who wrote as follows: 'I arrived in Switzerland the day before Graham died and I stayed with Yvonne for a week. I left after the funeral. We talked all through the days and late into the nights. She showed me her little red book in which she had kept a record of her conversations with Graham and in which he had also made notes next to her writing. Before I left she gave me this little piece from the book to take back to my mother [Elisabeth]. It is one of the notes Graham made in the book. It reads, "I would add that perhaps in Paradise we are given the power to help the living. I picture Paradise as a place of activity. Sometimes I pray not *for* the dead friends but *to* dead friends, asking their help."' M.-F.A.

there was a blood problem which could be controlled with the help of transfusions. This was in the winter of 1989–90.

That, alas, was the beginning of a long period which became a nightmare for him. And yet he was still able to make the occasional joke: 'What is it I'm suffering from?' he asked one day. We were in his flat, and he was in bed. 'Anaemia or amnesia?'

For someone like him, who had retained all his vivacity and wit, and who, as you can see, was conscious and lucid enough to be able to make puns, it was an utterly wretched time. He was not in pain, but his life depended on these regular transfusions, which were done once a fortnight. He told me that he felt 'like a prisoner attached to his chains'.

As long as he could hope that it was a passing phase, he accepted the situation. But as time went by and there was no improvement, he began to have had enough and he wanted to be finished with it. There was nothing more that could be done. His body was rejecting the transfusions. He was perfectly aware of this, and not only did he accept it, but it gave him enormous comfort. I feel tempted to say 'like a gift from God'. His mind was clear, and he experienced and faced up to death with great lucidity and, I would say, even greater courage. But he was in a hurry for it to be over.*

Soizic: It doesn't seem to have been quite the 'serenity' you mentioned earlier.

Yvonne: That was to do with another, specific kind of serenity:

---

* See the very detailed and interesting work done by Pierre Smolik on Graham Greene's visits to Switzerland and, in particular, on his final moments. Smolik put together certain statements made by Yvonne, which corroborate all that she had told me, among them the following: 'Greene would make it known, in full knowledge of the facts, that he wished to go peacefully and therefore asked that both the investigations and the transfusions be discontinued. From then on they just made sure that he was well cared for.' Pierre Smolik, 'Graham Greene et la Suisse', in *Vibiscum, Annales veveysannes*, no. 7, p. 155, Vevey, 1999; certain passages have been annotated by Yvonne, notably: 'He left no specific message on his bedside table.'

serenity in the face of death. For he had certainly got rid of his anguish, the famous anguish, which he also talked to you about once, in *The Other Man* (he was just recovering from an illness which could have been fatal, but you didn't know that), when he said that it is 'the hope of survival that generates anguish, for anguish lies in the conflict between the hope of surviving and the fear of not surviving'. Now, in this case, quite clearly, impatience had taken the place of hope – another basic feature of his character. From that moment on, he was 'in a hurry to be gone'. It's curious, what's more, for at that moment his lack of patience reappeared very forcibly – even though he was physically very weak.

I realised then that the end was near. I wept.*

My daughter, Martine, who lived a hundred yards from us at Châno, had just left the hospital. It was the first of April. I can remember their conversation, which was completely normal. Martine said to Graham, trying to comfort him, 'All the same, Graham, you must admit you've had a very full life, and you've written some marvellous books.' Graham, who was never satisfied with himself, said, 'A few, yes, are good books. Perhaps people will think of me from time to time, as they think of Flaubert.' In 1979, you remember, he said almost the same thing . . . Mind you, he liked Flaubert.

And then, once again, we were alone in that hospital room. 'Why does it take so long coming?' he sighed. He was taking leave of me . . . The two of us were there and we were talking to each other. He was already speaking about himself in the past. I said, 'But you're still here, we're still together!' And then he pushed me away. I took his hands. He pushed me away with his hands, and he said with a gesture almost of . . . not anger, but . . .

Soizic: Impatience?

---

* When I saw Yvonne again at Graham's burial, in the cemetery at Corseaux, she, who was in any case very petite, was a shadow of herself. She must have lost about ten kilos.

Yvonne: Yes. He said, 'But I want to go.' He pushed me away. 'But I want to go.' That upset me deeply. I was shattered. It was tough, very tough. But now, when I look back, I tell myself that he appeared to be hard, but it was for my own good. Perhaps he meant it to mean, 'Well, when I'm gone, you can say to yourself that it was I who wanted to go.' It may have been a reflex. A rational reflex, even though it seemed harsh, paradoxical and contradictory. He wanted to release me from all blame – so that I could say to myself, 'Well, he wanted to go.' At the time I was hurt, but deep down it was a consolation. Death – he no longer had the patience to wait for it. He wanted to go.

So then I hoped that it would come quickly.

Earlier that day, I had indeed suggested summoning his friend, the Spanish priest Leopoldo Durán. He raised his hand casually and said, 'Oh, if you want to . . .' That implied that he was indifferent.

Soizic: As a priest or as a friend?

Yvonne: Both, I think. A little earlier, at Châno, he had been visited by Father Cuzon, the Catholic priest in Vevey, who liked Graham so much and was so impressed by him that he told him his entire life story, forgetting to suggest that he hear his confession, but I don't think that Graham was thinking about this at that moment.

'But I want to go' were his last words.

By the next day he had fallen into a coma. He died on Wednesday, the third of April, at 11.40 a.m.

Soizic: Were you there at the moment when he passed away?

Yvonne: I was in the Vevey hospital. I had gone to telephone Michelle Lapautre,* so that she could alert Robert Laffont – I didn't want Robert to hear of his death through the newspapers. The nurse had told me it was a matter of hours. His breathing

---

* Michelle Lapautre, Graham's literary agent in Paris. Both she and her husband, René, were friends of Graham's and were present at his funeral.

was heavy. I didn't want to see him. The nurse caught up with me, put her hand on my shoulder, and said, 'There, it's over.' It's strange when I think back on how I felt at that moment. A mixture of despair and relief. Relief, certainly. You become a sort of robot whose physical strength is running down while at the same time a huge void is forming in your head with just one idea in mind: to hold on till the end.

Soizic: What was the worst moment for either of you?

Yvonne: It was that winter – the winter of 1990 – just after Christmas. I had gone to see him, as I did every day when he was in hospital, and all of a sudden an expression came over his face . . . the expression of an upset child, perhaps – but certainly that of a child [*Yvonne showed how Graham seized her hands and her wrists tightly*] and he said, 'I love you; you know how much I love you.' And he burst into tears. He turned his head away. It was the only time I saw him cry. He was really weeping. And shaking with emotion. I had often seen his eyes moisten, but this time genuine tears were flowing.

And then he pulled himself together. 'Why am I crying? I can't remember having cried since I was a child.'

I stayed with him a little while longer, but after that I found it hard, very hard. I think that was the worst moment. I told myself I couldn't outlive him, and I was frightened of doing something silly.

I left the hospital. I came here, to Châno. I can't say what sort of state I was in. I was in despair.

That was the day he said goodbye to me, the day I realised what was happening.

In my heart of hearts I almost hoped that it would come quickly, because I told myself: I must hold on till the end, I must help him right up to the end.

I arrived at Châno. I told myself that the only person who would understand me would be his daughter Caroline. I phoned her. She knew that things were going badly. She came at once. I must say that I shall never forget what she did. It helped me recover myself. She stayed for a good while. We drank two glasses of whisky. We talked. Well, about all that . . .

I think that moment was really worse than death itself, because until then I hadn't believed it would happen . . . For me, he was immortal. He would never be out of my sight. And then I realised, yes, that he was saying goodbye to me.

Soizic: Would you say that for him the thought of having to leave you was worse than the prospect of death?

Yvonne: Graham was a man who had an acute sense of responsibility. Towards everyone. He left nothing to chance and never neglected anything. For example, before his death he handed me the letters Sir John Cairncross wrote to him, so that I could return them. Right up to the end, he was terribly worried about what would become of me, and so considerate. At the hospital in Vevey, when I was crying one day, he said, 'I understand that you are sad, but I don't want you to be depressed.' By the way, notice how careful and precise he always was in his choice of words, the distinctions he made, and how concerned he always was for the other person. At Châno once, shortly before his death, looking at me with great tenderness, he came up to me – I was sitting down – and said, 'You look so tired. I'm worried about you.' While he himself was dying, virtually.

Soizic: But you did look very tired.

Yvonne: He didn't just express this care for others in words. On the last journey between Antibes and Vevey – it was at the end of 1990 (we stayed together at Châno for a year and a half) – when he was getting off the plane at Vevey airport, Graham handed me an envelope. It contained a cheque and a little note: 'In case anything happens to me.' After a few days, I tore the cheque up.

Soizic: What was his expression like when he gave you the envelope?

Yvonne: Not sad. Neutral. It showed that he was aware of his condition, yet at the same time he didn't want to alarm me unduly. This leads me to respond to your original question about fear of death and separation. He said to me several times, 'I'm not afraid of death. What I'm afraid of is being separated from you.'

Soizic: At what stage of his illness did he say that?

Yvonne: Shortly before the end, mostly. I remember one conversation. He had said again, 'What I am afraid of is being separated from you.' So I reassured him: 'But I will come and join you.' Graham: 'Yes, but it will take a long time.' I remember answering, 'You won't know, because time won't exist for you any more.' He looked at me, with a blank look: 'Then, poor you . . .' Which proves that he trusted in my love.

Soizic: But that he hadn't yet assimilated the notion of the non-existence of time after death?

Yvonne: He found it impossible to understand that notion, because he attached a great deal of importance to time. For example, whenever we went to Providence Hospital, for his transfusions or for tests to be carried out, and I asked him, 'What do you want me to put in your case?' he replied (and this was always the first thing he mentioned), 'The black clock.' Always the little black alarm clock. It just happened to be black, but that's nothing to do with it. What mattered was to know the time. To know what he was doing.

More than death, he was frightened of 'extinction'. He mentioned this in *A World of My Own*, in the last chapter:

In the dream I had been aware of people I had loved who called me to join them. But I had chosen, by my lack of belief, extinction. A great black cone like a candle extinguisher was to be dropped over my head.

In the discussion that followed, I argued that we all, whatever our beliefs, feared extinction.

Yet despite the paradoxes and doubts, and the antinomic aspects of him, I don't have the feeling that this fear was present before his death. No, what struck all those who came to see him was his calmness. He was exceptionally calm. For example, just after Graham died, I remember having a conversation with Dr Morandi, the doctor who had been treating him, and he told me, 'I have never come across such a case before. Normally, whatever the age, whatever the illness, patients are afraid of death. They fight, they cling to life, they panic. No sign of this with Mr Greene.' 'How do you explain that?' I asked. 'I attribute it to his intelligence,' the doctor said, 'his exceptional intelligence.' Those were his words.

Yes, certainly, he was highly intelligent, but I don't think that that is enough to explain an attitude such as his. I believe he succeeded in ridding himself of his anguish by giving himself over entirely to emptiness . . .

Soizic: What do you mean by that?

Yvonne: After his death, in his study, I found an undated poem in his handwriting. I only managed to decipher it in snatches. Read it, Soizic.

Soizic: 'The tall houses along the quai/ seem as grey/ as the mood/ of those who remember a certain February/ perhaps, a certain December/ when the same Paris was not empty/ as in a day called today./ The bar of the Ritz was full,/ and the place Vendôme was full,/ and the rue St Honoré was full . . .' (Then I can't decipher the next bit) '. . . and the shoppers around . . . how empty our existence . . .'

Yvonne: Do you see how meaningful he makes emptiness appear?*

Soizic: But, now confronted with death, where did faith fit into all of this? Greene the Catholic? The agnostic?

Yvonne: The man who wasn't a saint . . . clearly.

Soizic: That reminds me of his remark to you about your grandmother: 'But your grandmother was a saint.' Tell me about your grandmother; the story sheds such light on Graham's last moments.

Yvonne: Well, towards the end of her life, my grandmother lived with us at my mother's house, at the station – my mother was the stationmaster – at Tal Ar Groaz, which in Breton means 'at the foot of the cross'. In fact, there was no mystical connotation; it was simply that there were two main roads which crossed, with signposts indicating directions to neighbouring towns. My grandmother, sensing that she did not have long to live, asked to see a priest. She was very devout. So my mother asked the village priest to come and see her. But one day my grandmother started saying to my mother, 'Ah, if only you would come with me, I'd be happy to go.' To begin with, my mother didn't react. But she went on and on. Until one day my mother said to her, 'You know I've got three children to bring up. I can't just go like that and leave three children behind.' They spoke entirely in Breton, for my grandmother didn't speak a word of French. Finally, my mother said, 'What difference does it make to you whether I'm there or not? Why is it so important to you?' Mam goz replied, 'You know, I can't read and I'm frightened of making a mistake. I'm going to arrive at a crossroads and in one direction it'll say Hell, and in the other, Heaven, and I might take the wrong

* According to Yvonne, this poem appears in various places, notably in the catalogue that Nick Dennys compiled of the books in Graham's library.

road.' For her there was no doubt that she would go to heaven –
and I'm sure she went there directly, for she deserved to.

Graham listened to this story and I suddenly saw that he had
tears in his eyes. When I had finished telling it to him, he was
silent, and then he said, 'You should pray to your grandmother,
you know, you should address prayers to her, for she is a saint.'
And she was a saint.

Soizic: Do you think that in his final moments his serenity,
which astonished everyone, was somehow close to your grandmother's attitude?

Yvonne: No, he certainly didn't have the assurance, the innocence or calm acceptance that Mam goz had. Throughout this
difficult period, he was conscious of the wall in front of him. But
that quiet certainty . . . No he didn't really have that. It was rather
more like the state of mind of the poet Unamuno, whom he
admired and whom he felt close to in his paradoxical search for
God. He quoted him, notably in *Ways of Escape*, and I often
heard him say, 'Those who believe that they believe in God, but
without passion in their hearts, without anguish of mind, without
uncertainty, without doubt, without an element of despair in
them, in their consolation, believe only in the "God" idea, not in
God Himself.' I sometimes used to discuss this, after Graham's
death, with my friend the priest Alberto Huerta. It was something
Graham himself felt. It could equally well apply to him, too.

Yet when he used to say to me, 'I love you for ever and the
longest day', he believed in it. It was that: life eternal. If he hadn't
believed it, he wouldn't have said it, and so often, too. Throughout our entire life together, he never lied to me, and he never made
promises he didn't keep. And so I say to myself, 'Why would he
have betrayed himself, just over this?' It makes no sense.

17

'In My End is My Beginning'
(Mary, Queen of Scots, as quoted by Yvonne)

Graham is buried in the little cemetery at Corseaux. Apparently, he chose the spot, and he told Ruth Lazarus, 'This is the place for me.' It was a good choice. Not far from his daughter Caroline's house, and close to Châno. Yvonne often used to visit and place flowers on his grave, which she carefully maintained almost to the end of her own life. I often accompanied her. One day in 1997, standing by the tombstone, she took out her lipstick and began to make herself up. Seeing my look of surprise, she told me with a mysterious smile that it was really meant for Graham: 'He liked the taste of lipstick.' I don't know exactly where she is buried – where her own ashes are. In my imagination, she may have been infringing the social and religious etiquette that she adhered to during her life. And yet I had witnessed her own pathetic diffidence, on the day Graham was buried, when I had to push her forward – the companion of so many years – in order that she dare, though only after family and friends had done so, bless the coffin of the man she had never deserted.

She cared passionately about this work of testimony, this memoir. I have had to complete it without her being present to make any final alterations, but I have not added or removed a word, nor, indeed, have I embellished any of the information she confided to me and which I believe she wished me to divulge. Naturally, with the imposing amount of basic material that we had assembled, I sometimes regret we did not use it all. But to say or reveal any more would be to betray her and Graham. And everyone else, too. His readers. It would be a fraudulent piece of work. When all is said and done, this love story belongs to Graham and Yvonne, and the spirit that emerges from it – that alone – belongs to his readers, to his work. Not to have contributed to a distortion of his work, but to have contributed to providing a glimpse of the 'other man', one who was disarmingly tender and loving: that is what Yvonne has given us. Because that is the woman she was.

Soizic: You often asked him, 'How much do you love me?' And that's when he would reply, 'I love you, for ever and a day . . . for ever and the longest day', but why the question?

Yvonne: It had to do with a fear of losing him. The only way I could imagine losing him was through death.

Soizic: Do you feel as if you have lost him, now?

Yvonne: No. But it's as if everything was extinguished with him. I'm alone in this flat [at Châno], and I keep thinking I'll see him turn up in the corner of a room . . .

Soizic: And yet I wouldn't say that Yvonne Cloetta is someone who lives in the past.

Yvonne: Within myself, I do.

Soizic: It doesn't seem that way.

Yvonne: But a past adapted to the present. In my mind, he's still very much present. I miss him, but I'm not looking for compensation. I don't even think of it.

Soizic: Do you mean 'compensation' as far as eventual other men may be concerned? Over thirty years, you may perhaps have been attracted to other men, no?

Yvonne [*laughing*]: No, no, indeed not . . . Well, you know . . . I'm even surprised myself. From the moment he entered my life, I never looked at men in the same way. Not once. Over thirty years.

 I'm thinking of that friend who came yesterday in all innocence. I said to him, 'Graham will be the last. Graham was the best. He will be the best and the last.' And that's how it's going to be, I know.

Soizic: Doesn't it hurt?

Yvonne: Yes, it hurts. I miss him terribly. But the idea of another man touching me: no. You know, when you're crazy about someone, it's so entrenched, it's so profound. That doesn't mean I don't have male friends, but . . .

Soizic: Aren't you tempted, even fleetingly?

Yvonne: No.

Soizic: Do you ever dream about other men?

Yvonne: Not at all. I very rarely dream about Graham, incidentally. I think about him. Every day. The absence is unbearable, but the work you and I do helps me to root out the pain a little, shall we say. And yet I'm torn between a deep desire to keep everything about the life we had together jealously to myself, and at the same time a need to express it all. I don't like writing . . . I've got piles of scraps of paper, thoughts that came to me like that . . . I kept this little diary, my *Carnet rouge*, which he used to look at, read and annotate, but now, knowing he can no longer add his comments, I'm suddenly far less interested. It would now be one-way traffic.

Soizic: Do you think you'll see the end of this work we're putting together, casting light on thirty-two years of shared life? It's very long. We can't spend years talking about everything. Do you think you'll manage to say everything?

Yvonne: No, surely not. Firstly, I won't have enough time, and then . . . expressing it . . . No.

Soizic: Do you select what you want to describe?

Yvonne: No, because there are two of us doing it. But when you leave and I remember what it is I still want to say, it turns out differently. For there is so much to shed light on. It's not possible. We'd need whole days and nights to express everything about our lives together.

When we're together, you and I, what I feel I want to say is that I was extraordinarily lucky to have met him and to have kept him for so long. I don't always make that clear. At school in Quimper, when I was a teenager, for example, we were told about Monte Carlo. At the time, it was a sort of paradise which was so far away and so beyond me that I never expected I would see it one day. But then, to think that I could meet a man like Graham . . .

Soizic: *La petite bretonne.* The little Breton girl?

Yvonne: Yes, the little Breton girl came out of her shell.

Soizic: Do you think he had a special affection for you precisely because you were this little Breton girl?

Yvonne: No. It was physical. It was a passion that can't be explained in detail. That's how it was and there's nothing more to be said. We were happy together and we didn't try to analyse our relationship.

Soizic: Did Catholicism draw you closer to one another?

Yvonne: I would say that it didn't pose any problems, in the sense that I have always thought that a love like that could only be a gift from God and that I didn't have the right to refuse it. Religion for me was something similar to my love for him. I said to myself: to refuse would be an offence to God. It may be a philosophy that suited me, but that's how it was . . .

Soizic: Which of you loved the other more?

Yvonne: I can't answer that question. I know what I myself felt. I don't know what *he* felt. For with love it's not a question of words. Neither is it quantifiable. I said this to him time and again. It's a whole way of behaviour, the little everyday things one does. The way he behaved towards me. Now in that respect he really was irreproachable. There's nothing more I can say; as far as that goes, he was irreproachable.

Soizic: You spoke to me about the 'enveloping' nature of his love. Without being too indiscreet, can I ask you to give a few examples of that?

Yvonne: Yes. Well, I hope he would not have been annoyed with me for telling you this. He did say to me that, should such a book come out after his death, 'Either you speak, or you say nothing.' One night, when I was on the point of falling asleep, I heard this soft, very gentle voice whispering, 'Are you asleep, darling?' He wanted to make sure that I was properly asleep, because he could never fall asleep before me.

Soizic: Really? Every night?

Yvonne: Of course. Because after that night I, too, wanted to find out, so on certain nights I used to make my breathing heavy and regular. And every time I did so, he would say the same thing. One night I asked, 'Aren't you tired? Don't you want to go to sleep?'* He replied, 'I fight against it, but I want to make sure that you're asleep before I go to sleep.'

Soizic: And he did this for thirty years, virtually?

Yvonne: Yes, it's incredible. Here you have the man who some people said was cruel to women! Naturally, I sometimes fell asleep and did not hear him, but as far as I know he must have said it every night.

Soizic: And in the morning, when you woke, what did he do?

Yvonne: Make love, mostly [*laughing*]!
   It was wonderful. All that could be expected of a man, he gave me – and more. More than I could ever have hoped for. You see, to return to the *lycée* at Quimper for a moment, when we girls spoke among ourselves about our ideal man, the man we most wanted to meet, for me he always had to be tall, dark, with blue eyes and . . . a clerk! A clerk, probably because that represented security. That's what I wanted. But he didn't exactly give me that!

Soizic: Nevertheless, Graham must surely have represented enormous security for you? Someone who showed so much affection, and so much desire, too. You had both.

Yvonne: I felt so protected. It's one of the things I suffered from most after he had gone. Suddenly, his death was like a storm

* In French Yvonne used the contracted, interrogative form: '*t'es pas*' or '*t'as pas*', denoting great affection.

which blew through my life, and afterwards I felt totally destitute. Everything had gone. It was worse than a storm. Something which destroys everything. I was naked. Completely disoriented. You know, I wonder how I managed to get through that period.

Soizic: He hasn't disappeared from your life, in fact. He has disappeared without disappearing, which is worse, isn't it?

Yvonne: No, but you see, unless you've been through this you can't understand. Yes, he has disappeared without disappearing, but within me he's always present, that's certain, and he will remain there.

Soizic: Do you think your period of mourning for Graham is over, though?

Yvonne: What exactly do you mean by that?

Soizic: The business of coming to terms with death.

Yvonne: Well, I understand what it means, if you like. But for me, after everything he said to me, I harbour the hope of finding him again. How, I don't know. I don't imagine the sort of scene in which someone says, 'Hello, it's me,' but something of the kind. How, I don't know.

Soizic: So you believe in this 'longest day'?

Yvonne: Yes, well, I do believe in it, it's true. It's the only thing that keeps me going. Otherwise, I'd have said goodbye to everything . . .
    Naturally, nothing is as it was before, that's obvious. But if I didn't retain this hope of finding him again, I'd collapse into despair and I'd be devastated, because everything would go to

pieces. But I don't want things to go to pieces. I don't want to let myself go. It's a struggle against myself.

Soizic: You owe him that, and you also owe it to yourself.

Yvonne: Absolutely. When I get desperate I think of him, and then I say to myself, 'He wouldn't want that.' So I have to keep going. Continually. It's a moral duty. You feel like giving up, but it's more than a duty, it's an objective. But you know, by and large, he gave me so much that it's quite natural I should now miss it all horribly. It's logical, obvious. Considering all the happiness he gave me . . . Throughout all those years that happiness became almost 'normal', almost natural.

It's now that I no longer have him that I realise how lucky I have been, and that perhaps I should have done more for him.

Soizic: Why? Done more in what way?

Yvonne: I don't know . . . Well, it hasn't exactly been a 'normal' life, but I have absolutely no regrets, on either the positive or the negative side. I don't regret not having made the decision to divorce in order to live entirely with him, because that would have meant making sacrifices on my part – sacrifices as far as my daughters were concerned particularly and I know that I would never have forgiven myself, either. And that would have spoiled our relationship.

But there is one thing I do regret: not having realised that the end was near, and not having come to live here at Corseaux for longer, but, well, that's not important.

Soizic: One can't foresee the end, in any case.

Yvonne: No, of course. You can't know when it's going to happen. All the time we lived in Antibes I never ever believed it would. He worked every morning, as he always did, right up to the end. On his book of dreams. He, who was haunted by the thought of not being able to write, who used to say, 'I'm afraid of living too long away from writing'; it's as if his wishes were granted. That's a consolation, at least. It was not until the doctor who was treating him, Dr Sirvin, said to me one day, 'You know, it's really not very sensible, at this stage, to leave him alone at night' (I was sleeping at Juan-les-Pins), that I packed a bag. I took the decision to come to Corseaux on the spur of the moment . . . Yes, I should have persuaded him to come and live in Switzerland sooner so that we could spend all our time together.* But on the other hand, he liked his little flat in Antibes; he needed his solitude to work a few hours each day. And as for me, I still hoped that he would live longer. I knew he wouldn't get better, but I didn't realise that the end was so near. It should also be said that Corseaux in winter is a bleak place. In January 1991, for example, there was lots of snow. The roads were icy. One day Graham, who was climbing the slope that led up to our building, fell flat on his face. I tried to pick him up, but he was very heavy. I couldn't manage. It was a nightmare. Eventually, with the help of neighbours, we were able to get him to his feet. But I was terrified that it would happen again.

Fortunately, since I am a believer, I can fall back on this goal: finding him again. I recall the words of the Trappist monk Ralph Rite: 'The past does not come back, but neither does it disappear. Perhaps this is due to the fact that we all have an

---

* Graham's white towelling dressing-gown was still hanging there, in one of the bathrooms, in 2000. One day, I caught a glimpse of Yvonne, through the half-open bedroom door. She was asleep, taking up only a small portion of their large bed . . . I have inherited Graham's toaster. It was broken, and Yvonne was going to get rid of it. She often described to me how Graham prepared his toast for breakfast, standing and watching over this infernal object, which had no means of ejecting slices when they were ready . . . Hundreds of tiny details brought him back to life, not counting his favourite paintings or sculptures.

element of eternity in our souls.' At Corseaux I became friendly with a priest, Father Cuzon, whom I spoke to you about. He came here, to the flat. I asked him to say mass in memory of Graham on the first anniversary of his death, for a few friends. There were the MacCulloughs, our neighbours, and Caroline – five or six of us, not more. Afterwards, Father Cuzon came up to me and said, 'And you, how are you coping? You have to be strong, you have to fight. One's got to carry on.' I replied, 'You see, for me it's the thought of never seeing him again, never hearing him again, never being able to touch him again, that I find so unbearable.' He then said, 'You're a Catholic: you're not allowed to say that. Death is a beginning, not an end.' That has helped me enormously.

It's not the great things we did together, it's the day-to-day life, sharing all one's impressions. Being able to say everything to him. That's what I miss so much. It's dreadful, you know.

Yvonne picked up her *Carnet rouge* and read some words of Graham's she had written down: 'It's at railway stations that you notice people who love each other. They're always the last on the platform, waving their handkerchiefs as the train carrying their loved one sets off.' In a whisper, she added, 'I hoped that I would be the last one left on the platform.'

She continued her reading: 'I now realise that love – real, true love – between two human beings only reveals itself once it's no longer a question of sex.' Choking a little, she murmured, 'It's hard, you know . . .'

Later on, the summer before she died, at Juan-les-Pins, in the weakest of voices she sighed, 'At least when I go, I'll go to meet him.'

Afterword

Max Reinhardt died in November 2002, a year after Yvonne's death. He and his wife Joan met Yvonne at Saint-Jean-Cap-Ferrat in the summer of 1959, when Graham invited Yvonne to join him following their meeting in Douala earlier that year. The four of them became firm friends. They met every summer at Saint-Jean-Cap-Ferrat, where Max kept a small boat, and also periodically in London. When, after Graham's death, Yvonne told Max of her plans for this book he was enthusiastic and urged her to go ahead. He continued to support the project when at times, to Yvonne, the task seemed overwhelming. That it is now complete is in no small measure thanks to Max and Joan Reinhardt's unfailing encouragement.

Marie-Françoise Allain

Acknowledgements

My warmest thanks for the completion of this task must go to my long-time friend Janet Cheng who helped me so much, firstly with the deciphering of the cassettes of *The Other Man* and now with this book. Euan Cameron has always been there, a precious translator, friend, I would almost say accomplice. Amanda Saunders, Graham's niece, granted us her talent with the startling photographs she took, and her competence in checking biographical facts. Bruce Hunter, our agent in London, has been in the background, fair and stern, in touch with Yvonne for almost ten years. I have had a real sense of good team-work at Bloomsbury: my thanks to Alexandra Pringle, Chiki Sarkar, and Mary Tomlinson. I will never forget the warm welcome of the Reinhardt house and their assistant Belinda McGill. Ruth Lazarus, Yvonne's good friend, gave us advice together with photos of Yvonne. Pierre Joannon, one of Graham's companions in Antibes, sent stimulating encouragements. Brigitte Lehner, Yvonne's daughter, so close to her mother and father, has been an easy-going intermediary. I miss her sister Martine, often there in Switzerland when I was working with her mother. Today, I'm grateful to Philippe Landeau de Dié for his patience and fidelity . . .

Marie-Françoise Allain

Paris, November 2003

A NOTE ON THE TYPE

The text of this book is set in Linotype Sabon, named after the type founder, Jacques Sabon. It was designed by Jan Tschichold and jointly developed by Linotype, Monotype and Stempel, in response to a need for a typeface to be available in identical form for mechanical hot metal composition and hand composition using foundry type.

Tschichold based his design for Sabon roman on a font engraved by Garamond, and Sabon italic on a font by Granjon. It was first used in 1966 and has proved an enduring modern classic.